T0270963

The Digital Prism

Many people are concerned about the unchecked powers of tech giants and the hidden operations of big data and algorithms. Yet we do not have the vocabularies to properly articulate how these digital transformations shape our lives. This book shows how the management of our digital footprints, visibilities and attention is a central force in the digital transformation of societies and politics. Seen through the prism of digital technologies and data, the lives of people and workings of organizations take new shapes in our understanding. Making sense of these requires that we push beyond common ways of thinking about transparency and surveillance, and look at how managing visibilities is a central but overlooked phenomenon that influences how people live, how organizations work and how societies and politics operate.

MIKKEL FLYVERBOM is Professor of Communication and Digital Transformations and Academic Director of the research platform Digital Transformations at Copenhagen Business School. He is also Research Fellow at the Center for Information Technology and Society at University of California, Santa Barbara, a columnist for the Danish newspaper Politiken and widely used expert on tech issues. He is the author of *The Power of Networks: Organizing the Global Politics of the Internet* (2011).

The Digital Prism

Transparency and Managed Visibilities in a Datafied World

MIKKEL FLYVERBOM

Copenhagen Business School

CAMBRIDGE
UNIVERSITY PRESS

CAMBRIDGE
UNIVERSITY PRESS

University Printing House, Cambridge CB2 8BS, United Kingdom

One Liberty Plaza, 20th Floor, New York, NY 10006, USA

477 Williamstown Road, Port Melbourne, VIC 3207, Australia

314-321, 3rd Floor, Plot 3, Splendor Forum, Jasola District Centre, New Delhi - 110025, India

79 Anson Road, #06-04/06, Singapore 079906

Cambridge University Press is part of the University of Cambridge.

It furthers the University's mission by disseminating knowledge in the pursuit of education, learning and research at the highest international levels of excellence.

www.cambridge.org
Information on this title: www.cambridge.org/9781107130814
DOI: 10.1017/9781316442692

First published 2019

A catalogue record for this publication is available from the British Library

Library of Congress Cataloging in Publication data
Names: Flyverbom, Mikkel, author.
Title: The digital prism : transparency and visibility in the age of total information /
Mikkel Flyverbom.
Description: New York : Cambridge University Press, 2019.
Identifiers: LCCN 2019008717| ISBN 9781107130814 (hardback) | ISBN
9781107576964 (paperback)
Subjects: LCSH: Information society – Social aspects. | Information technology –
Management. | Electronic surveillance. | BISAC: BUSINESS & ECONOMICS /
Organizational Behavior.
Classification: LCC HM851 .F593 2019 | DDC 303.48/33–dc23
LC record available at https://lccn.loc.gov/2019008717

ISBN 978-1-107-13081-4 Hardback
ISBN 978-1-107-57696-4 Paperback

Contents

Acknowledgments

Books, like many other rewarding parts of life, are demanding, time consuming and sometimes painful. As much as I've enjoyed writing this book, it has also surprised me how difficult it is to carve out time and space for this kind of work. Often, more urgent issues would require my attention, and the pressure to focus on other kinds of publications seems to be mounting, at least in some circles. Still, I've been thrilled about the project, and I believe that books allow us to put together our thoughts and ideas in more elaborate and exploratory ways. They allow for ventures that journal articles do not permit. This book is one such venture, and a bit on roller skates, bringing together big discussions about digital transformations, transparency and visibilities, and travelling across levels of analysis such as the individual, the organizational and the societal. My hope is that these reflections will resonate with those of others – in academia, policy-making and the broader public – who are concerned with the intersection of technology and data and social life, particularly when it comes to what we come to see, know and act on when much of what we do happens in digital spaces. These are massive topics and will require much more work, and I'm thoroughly thrilled to see so much research and public discussion of technology issues. Finally, it seems that we are ready to explore the interface of technology and society. So much work has focused on technology itself – the next big thing that will change everything – and overlooked the human, organizational and societal forces that make some technological possibilities useless or even harmful. I'm happy that we see more nuanced and balanced approaches to these issues, because they will help us make wiser choices about technological and human developments, and I feel fortunate to have engaged with some of the people at the forefront of setting more reflective and critical agendas for our engagement with digital transformations. Writing this book would not have been possible without the many people, the many ideas and the many places that helped it come into being.

This book is the culmination of a long-standing interest in transparency as a recipe for organizational and social change. Luckily, many others are interested in questions about the effects of sharing information and opening up, and I want to thank some of them. At Copenhagen Business School, I am fortunate to be surrounded by smart and supportive colleagues, such as Dan Kärreman, Hans Krause Hansen, Lars Thøger Christensen, Julie Uldam, Dennis Schoeneborn, Christina Garsten and many others who have helped me develop and articulate these ideas about transparency and visibilities. In particular, my collaborations with Hans Krause Hansen, Lars Thøger Christensen and Oana Brindusa Albu on the topic of transparency paved the way for this book.

This book also benefitted from a Google Research Award that both allowed me to spend a semester at Stanford University and gave me very useful contacts inside Google and other tech companies in Silicon Valley in the early phases of the project. I am particularly grateful for the support from Vinton Cerf, one of the fathers of the internet and "Chief Internet Evangelist" and Vice-President at Google. My ideas and insights about the workings of transparency in and around tech companies have been shaped by valuable conversations with policy directors, policy managers and higher-level staff at Google in Mountain View, CA; at Facebook in Palo Alto and its new headquarters in Menlo Park, CA; and with Facebook and Google employees located in Europe. Also, I have used material from these tech companies' blogs and other public sources, and followed their participation in public meetings, hearings, news stories and events.

In later phases of writing, a Fulbright grant and a position as research fellow at Rutgers University with colleagues Craig Scott, Jack Bratich, Mark Akhus and others gave me both useful insights and the time to focus. Similarly, I have benefitted from valuable discussions with people at Microsoft Research, such as Tarleton

Gillespie, Nancy Baym, Sarah T. Hamid and Kate Crawford, and members of the KIN Center for Digital Innovation in Amsterdam, including Marleen Huysmann, Natalja Laurey, Amanda Porter and others.

While writing this book, I have also been excited to be part of a growing community of scholars asking difficult questions about transparency, secrecy, surveillance, spectacles and other visibility practices. My collaborations with wonderful, bright people such as Clare Birchall, Cynthia Stohl, Michael Stohl, Paul Leonardi, Juliane Reinecke, Jeffrey Treem, Tim Kuhn, Leopold Ringel, Mark Fenster, Shiv Ganesh and Andrea Mubi Brighenti made this book possible. Also, I'm thankful for the solid research assistance I got from Kalina Staikova and Jacob Ørmen, both of whom are becoming accomplished academics, and for the support of my two editors at Cambridge University Press, Paula Parish and Valerie Appleby. Finally, my deepest gratitude goes to Ursula Plesner, whose clear thinking and solid loving shaped this book and continues to shape my life in the best possible ways.

Books are also made in places and my favorite writing spot turned out to be the New York Public Library, where this book seemed more willing to be written than anywhere else, and where I had some of my happiest moments working on it. In Copenhagen, another beautiful library known as the Black Diamond provided a similar refuge when other tasks, meetings and deadlines threatened the viability of this book.

Some of the points in this book have appeared in other form in articles in the *International Journal of Communication*, *Business & Society*, the *European Journal of Social Theory* and *International Political Sociology*, and in book chapters.

Introduction: The Transparency Formula

Created in a dorm room at Harvard University, Facebook was a simple website set up to compare two pictures of female students at a time, inviting fellow students to mark them as hot or not. Since then, the scope and ambitions of Facebook have expanded considerably. Here is what Mark Zuckerberg said about the role of Facebook at a meeting on the financial results of the company ten years later: "Next, let's talk about understanding the world. What I mean by this is that every day, people post billions of pieces of content and connections into the graph and in doing this, they're helping to build the *clearest model of everything there is to know in the world*" (Facebook, 2013, italics added).

This book is about the promise that digital technologies and data can help us understand everything in the world. The hope that digital transformations will create transparency and clarity has spread beyond Silicon Valley and shapes all sorts of discussions about technology, politics and society. Contemporary moves toward openness and transparency in corporate and political affairs, we are told, are a direct result of developments in the realm of digital technologies (Finel and Lord, 2002; Sifry, 2011). This hope for societal and political re-engineering through technology is driven by a belief in transparency as a panacea – a form of sunlight that will work as a disinfectant (Brandeis, 1913) on all societal illnesses – and has given rise to an increasingly institutionalized transparency movement consisting of organizations, corporate actors and activists peddling this ideal. This "triumph of transparency" (Braithwaite and Drahos, 2000) revolves around a belief in increased information and communication as a direct path to accountability, trust and legitimacy (Power, 1997; Garsten and de Montoya, 2008). That is, if information is shared, we can see everything, we can understand everything and we can take command of everything so that no bad behavior takes place. Such hopes about transparency rely on a simple and deceptive formula that equates information with clarity and considers more information as a direct path to accountability. However, as this book argues, they overlook what is a much more intricate and paradoxical relationship between digital transformations, transparency projects and organizational and regulatory effects (Hansen and Flyverbom, 2015).

The companies driving contemporary digital transformations are a good starting point for this book's attempt to problematize the transparency formula. Google prides itself as a driver of transparency. Its search engine makes the world's information available, the company has developed a work culture focused on openness and it pushes for more transparency in politics and societies broadly. However, the first thing you do when entering the Google headquarters in Silicon Valley is to sign a non-disclosure agreement stating that you cannot disclose any information afterwards, or even tell anyone about the agreement. Also, it is impossible to get information about the earnings of the company in specific countries, and no one at Google will talk about how user data is commercialized across the different services and projects that it develops. Digital transformations make it possible to see everything, but some things are kept in the dark, and many of the tech companies pushing for transparency prefer to remain out of sight.

Similarly, one of Facebook's promises is also transparency. This goes for the internal workings of the company, and the way it tells users that they can see and control the data they share via the platform. Questioned by the US Congress over the Cambridge Analytica scandal, Zuckerberg repeatedly stressed that Facebook users have "complete control" over their data. As he explained in response to the many Congressmen posing vague, but critical questions, all you need to do is go to the privacy settings and tools of your account, and you can decide what to share with whom. However, these user settings are only part of the story, and the very reason he was being questioned was that a wealth of user data travel in ways that users have not asked for, and have no way of seeing or controlling. Third parties can track and extract data. Facebook compiles data about users and their friends, even people not using Facebook, as well as from data brokers who can fill in the final gaps. So rather than transparency and control, users get an opportunity to manage the data they make visible on the front page. In contrast, Facebook's business model is based on extracting all data, and the company refuses to explain how it uses these data. Digital platforms like Facebook allow for extensive transparency in some areas, but also ways of limiting who can see and control what.

Also smaller tech companies are increasingly committed to transparency as a mission and core value. For instance, at the social media company Buffer, all emails can be seen by everyone, and employees can take as much vacation time as they want, as long as they tell everyone about it. As a result, people use the shared email service less and less, and switch to other ways of communicating. And hardly anyone goes on holiday, especially because employees can see that their bosses never take time off. Digital possibilities for increased transparency create not just more clarity and insight, but also the need for strategies for concealing and staying out of sight.

I start with these peeks into corporations engaging with transparency efforts to highlight the argument that this book pursues, namely that transparency is no simple matter of opening up and sharing information, but rather a matter of managing visibilities in careful and strategic ways. Tech companies and the digital transformations they pursue are, at one and the same time, very visible, secretive, transparent, hidden and open, and the curiosity about this paradox is central to the book. The pages to follow explore, conceptually and critically, these intersections of digital transformations and transparency, secrecy and other visibility practices and their consequences for individual, organizational and societal affairs.

DIGITAL TRANSFORMATIONS

Digital transformations shape our lives in myriad ways. The reliance on digital technologies and the internet, and the emergence of big data and artificial intelligence have widespread consequences for economic, cultural, political and social activities. At present, these discussions take a number of shapes and are marked by disagreements as to whether we should think of digital transformations as blessings or curses.

Early discussions of the invention and spread of the internet focused on the potentials for dialogue, expression and democratization offered by this open and inclusive communications platform. Suddenly, it seemed like established institutions and elites, such as governments, editors and corporations could be challenged, we would all have possibilities for expression, and information would be set free. Celebrations of this new space – often referred to as *cyberspace* – and its potentials often focused on the importance of keeping it separate from governmental and corporate interests. Today, both the promises and this separation seem like wishful thinking, particularly when we consider how governments rely on the internet for surveillance schemes and how large companies like Amazon, Google and Facebook seek to dominate large chunks of this space. But the depictions of the internet as a liberating force continue to shape many discussions. The emergence of social media and the spread of user-generated content reignited hopes about democratization and possibilities for free expression; however, at present, the picture seems murkier, and we have a growing focus on surveillance, corporate dominance and the negative effects of digital transformations. Especially the scope of US surveillance schemes exposed by Edward Snowden in 2013 propelled these discussions into the public domain. Surveillance, it turned out, was not a targeted or abnormal effort, but most governments' default approach to dealing with citizens' activities in digital spaces. These developments, including the largely hidden role of internet companies as suppliers of data for government surveillance schemes, such as that of the US National Security Agency, have also propelled discussions about the relationship between digital transformations and citizen rights. The key questions, it seems, are increasingly about the roles and responsibilities of tech giants and the way they both come to govern many spheres of social life, and are subjected to new forms of governance (Flyverbom, 2016a; Gillespie, 2017b).

Another key issue is that digital technology makes it easier than ever to collect, store and distribute information. In a largely digital world, searches for information, comments and messages and walks through the city produce vast amounts of digital traces that can be picked up and used again and again. Internet companies have access to mind-blowing amounts of data showing everything we do, care about and search for in digital spaces. In many ways, we have gone from a situation where information was scarce and expensive to store to a situation where information is abundant and easily stored (Mayer-Schönberger, 2009; Andrejevic, 2013). While processes of digitalization have been under way for a long time, a new development that we can think of as *datafication* (Mayer-Schönberger and Cukier, 2014) is increasingly important. Datafication means that many parts of social life take the shape of digital traces. Friendships become "likes" on Facebook, movements through the city produce extensive digital footprints in GPS-enabled devices, and our searches for information show what we value or wish for as individuals and societies. In combination with automated sorting mechanisms, such as algorithms and artificial intelligence, these massive streams of digital traces can be used to identify important patterns and inform decisions about anything from consumers to health conditions to criminal activities. The excitement surrounding these developments has been massive and, despite its fuzziness, the term *big data* has been taken on by the public, by companies and by politicians.

Increasingly, much of what we know about people, organizations and societies comes from digital sources. We are told that these developments will solve many of the problems that have always marked science, statistics and other ways of producing knowledge. Soon, we will have access to all or most of the data about a given phenomenon, and have consistent and neutral forms of intelligence that can give us exact answers. Finally, we will know everything and have unbiased answers to all our questions. Some have even suggested that we will no longer need theories and other types of structured explanations, because the digital evidence will speak for itself (Anderson, 2008), and some have expectations that we will have forms of superintelligence that do not require human interference (Good, 1965; Bostrom, 2014). At the same time, we are also increasingly concerned about the fate of the masses of data that result from our reliance on digital technologies. As automated forms of analysis and artificial intelligence weave into the governance of social affairs, such as crime, risk assessments and other kinds of decision-making, we need to consider what happens to our ways of running societies and securing fundamental rights. Datafication not only gives us more insights, but also makes it possible to keep track of people and regulate behavior in new and problematic ways.

As a result of these developments, another concern is how digital transformations lead to the disruption of established industries. Newspapers and media companies are losing their ways of creating revenue as contents become digital and largely free, and advertising becomes a primary competence and the core business model of internet companies such as Google and Facebook. Traditional taxi companies are losing the fight against the influx of cheaper Uber drivers working under less rigid forms of regulation. Similarly, the hotel industry and existing models of urban development are challenged by the possibilities for short-term rentals and new sources of income offered by Airbnb. These developments point to the gap between the conditions and approaches of established industries and the more unruly possibilities that digital transformations afford when it comes to new business models and ways of organizing our societies.

At present, the disruptive and possibly negative consequences of digital transformations are on the minds of scholars, policymakers and the wider public (Foer, 2017; Taplin, 2017). To grapple with these, we need to consider what it means that digital technologies – often developed and controlled by a few giant companies – are becoming the backbones of commercial, political, cultural and other social affairs. We used to think of digital technologies as simple tools, or as spaces that we could enter and leave again. Earlier accounts focused on how individuals, organizations and societies made use of digital technology and sought to capture what the implications of these uses were (Zuboff, 1988; Castells, 1996). How will work routines be altered as a result of new, automated production techniques? Will personal computers change the way we learn and think? And what happens to power relations when we start to rely on information and communication technologies that may challenge existing strategies, hierarchies and authorities? Such questions were important and relevant to ask when hardware, software and computer networks emerged as new tools to be taken up or rejected. However, digital technologies are no longer simply tools that we pick up to do a particular task or use to find a quicker way of working. They can no longer be put down, because they have merged with social life and become societal backbones, rather than tools at the periphery of what we do and are. We no longer go online – i.e. enter a new space – because we are already and almost always connected. These infrastructural developments have consequences for how we think about digital technologies and their relation to social life. It no longer makes sense to talk about cyberspace as an independent, separate sphere or to distinguish between online and offline activities. We are, as DeNardis and Musiana (2016: 19) put it, entering "an era of global governance *by* Internet infrastructure," and we need to consider what this entails and where it takes us, as individuals, organizations and societies.

THE POWERS OF TECH COMPANIES

At present, digital spaces are dominated by a small handful of tech companies, and we need to understand these commercial and technical forces. We can think of tech companies as powerful in a number of ways – as financially, technologically, politically and culturally potent. Certainly, tech giants exercise these forms of power. They are now among the most profitable companies in the world. Measured by market value, Apple, Google, Microsoft, Amazon and Facebook have surpassed the giants of the past, such as banks and energy companies (Economist, 2016). By leading technological innovation, these companies control large chunks of the internet and seek to build monopolies by crushing or acquiring competitors. As one of the key figures in Silicon Valley puts it, "competition is for losers" (Thiel, 2014) and tech companies pursue market dominance in aggressive ways. Tech companies also take on roles in politics and regulation, either by invitation as experts or innovators, or through their extensive lobbying efforts (Flyverbom, 2018). Furthermore, we are increasingly aware that tech companies shape cultural production through the tools and services they offer. For instance, digital platforms, and in particular Facebook, have become the primary gateway to news and other kinds of cultural products. This creates increased pressure on all sorts of content production, and the foundations of, for instance, newspapers seem to be eroding: People no longer need a subscription because a lot of content is circulated via digital platforms. Advertising revenue also ends up elsewhere, because the same digital platforms offer more agile and targeted ways of reaching customers and more elaborate ways of documenting the effectiveness and reach of their services. Without these financial pillars, quality journalism and news production are under pressure, and a lot of newspapers and similar companies are searching for new business models and ways of producing, distributing and extracting value from their work. Digital platforms also increasingly take on the role as archives and editors of social life. When Google publishes its yearly list of words we have searched for in the past year – aptly named Google Zeitgeist and later renamed Google Trends – it reflects what we focus on, value or want to know, as individuals and societies. It may come as no surprise that in 2016, Pokémon Go, iPhone 7 and Donald Trump made the top of the list of search terms. Or that in 2017, people were highly interested in iPhone X, Hurricane Irma and Harvey Weinstein.

These many and entangled forms of power are important, but not exhaustive of how tech companies shape social affairs. What media critics, such as Walter Lippmann, said about newspapers in the 1920s, also goes for digital platforms: they play an important part in controlling how we view the world. Because they focus on what people like and share most, popular phenomena like sensational news stories come to the fore, while more complex ones move in the background. The content policies and values of digital platforms set limits to what we see in the first place. Facebook's automatic deletion of Nick Ut's iconic photo of a naked Vietnamese girl fleeing the US napalm bombings is one example. The photo was uploaded first as part of a series of images that changed our perception of wars, and later by a Norwegian newspaper reporting on the story. In both cases, it was automatically identified as nudity, which clashes with the guidelines and policies of the platform, and taken down. The ensuing critique of Facebook's role as the "world's most powerful editor" censoring an important historical image highlighted how such companies increasingly shape public domains.

As they become our entry points for an increasing number of daily activities, digital platforms become intimately involved in editing and the ordering of social life. Without being very explicit about it, internet companies seek to become our gateways into whatever slice of social life they focus on, whether it is search, social relations, images, books or movies. From a business perspective, the ambition is obviously to become dominant in areas where they can gain access to more data and insights about people using their platform, and thus make it more difficult for competitors to gain a foothold. But the consequences of these attempts at carving out chunks of social life by offering infrastructures and services cut deeper. Facebook, for instance, is not interested in news as such, but as content that people are eager to click on and share. While the company has insisted that it is a technological utility, and not a media company, developments such as the deletion of the picture of the Vietnamese girl and the widespread circulation of "fake news" have increased the pressure for more reflections on the roles and responsibilities of digital platforms.

The power of tech companies extends beyond finances, technologies and politics. To grasp their significance, we need to include a focus on how they have access to information that was previously invisible or inaccessible, because it was controlled by corporations or individuals, and how they use such information to shape what we see and give attention to. There is a growing awareness that internet companies and technological innovation are mainly US phenomena. Also, questions about job creation, economic growth and taxes come up in many discussions about digital transformations. Internet companies and social media platforms may not be very labor intensive industries, but the concerns about the effects of Europe's poor performance in the digital domain are widespread. When internet giants operate outside the USA, Europe gets very few taxes and a small number of data centers with a minimum of local job openings. Related discussions of digital transformations focus on US cultural dominance. Because of the popularity and size of these companies, they can turn US values and standards into global ones. This often happens simply by demanding users to accept an overwhelming list of terms of service or through the adherence to community standards defining what can and cannot be shared or done on their platform (Gillespie, 2018b). On most social media sites, some forms of violence are acceptable, but no naked breasts, and free speech is balanced against concerns about discrimination and hatred. Contents and users that violate these standards simply disappear from the site, either through handheld or automated forms of content moderation. In itself, this is not at all surprising or controversial: internet companies, like all other companies, are free to make these decisions about what they want and do not want to accommodate. However, these digital platforms increasingly function as backbones for a wide number of human activities, such as building social relations, finding information or shaping cultural formations, and we need to consider their roles and responsibilities.

Digital technologies and tech companies do not simply transmit information, but also organize, order and transform societies. To appreciate the ordering capacities (Flyverbom, 2011) of digital transformations, we need to consider how technologies and data afford and constrain possibilities for action, but also produce particular ways of seeing, knowing and governing. This is why we need to focus on the management of visibilities. This extends and differs from the more well-known arguments that technologies have societal effects (Introna, 2007), like the creation of new forms of community, or that they can be used strategically to disrupt established approaches to politics. In their role as ubiquitous infrastructures, digital technologies are foundational mechanisms or operating systems (Peters, 2015) that filter and shape what we see and do not see, what we consider important and what we seek to control. The word *prism* in the title of this book alludes to this idea. Digital technologies are our eyes and gateways to the world.

Gillespie's (2014) work on algorithms addresses one aspect of this by pointing to the many ways in which automated decisions about categorization and sorting have relevance for social life. Like editors of newspapers, algorithms decide what is placed front and center and what is left out of sight. Only the kinds of information that are algorithm-ready get picked up, and we get the most popular points of view served up first. What comes out on top – in social relations, in culture and many other sorts of valuations – is increasingly a result of datafied processes and algorithmic operations. The starting point for this book is that digital technologies are fundamental to the production and circulation of data, information and knowledge, and that they guide our attention in particular directions and facilitate governance in significant ways. What I set out to show is that digitalization and datafication afford *visibility management* in new ways and to new degrees, and that these developments should be at the center when we grapple with the societal consequences of digital technologies and big data. But we need to start elsewhere and consider how different kinds of technological developments have been understood and conceptualized.

I summarize these broad discussions about digital transformations both to highlight their importance, and to hint at their limitations. Big data, algorithms and artificial intelligence are important topics. It is likewise important that we discuss the size, monopoly ambitions and market shares of big internet companies. But it also makes us overlook what I consider to be the most fundamental importance of digital transformations, namely that they make us see and know things in new ways. As digital platforms move closer and closer to the core of social and cultural life, we should also be asking questions about how *digital transformations shape how we see, know and govern social life.* These questions are about the relationship between digital transformations and what I term the *management of visibilities.* Compared to internet giants' size, financial advantages and number of users, these concerns are much more fuzzy and subtle. But they are central if we want to grasp the shape and consequences of contemporary digital transformations.

THE TRANSPARENCY FORMULA

One of the most dominant dreams about digital transformations is that they will give us access to perfect and total information – full transparency. Such hopes about digital technologies as facilitators and drivers of transparency shape contemporary life in all sorts of ways. States tell us they need extensive surveillance programs to prevent terrorist attacks, organizations promise to open their books and show us their insides, and fitness trackers offer us new ways of understanding our bodies and health conditions.

Accounts of this relationship between digital transformations and transparency take a number of distinct shapes: To some, digital technologies foster hopes about the positive effects of transparency for societal and organizational conduct. Consider, for instance, Sifry's (2011: 189) diagnosis that: "More information, plus the Internet's power to spread it beyond centralized control, is our best defense against opacity and the bad behavior it can enable." These developments promise to put an end to secrecy and centralized forms of power, because "we are living in an age of unprecedented transparency. Thanks to the revolution in information technology, the spread of democratic institutions, and the rise of global media, keeping secrets has become harder than ever before. These trends have distributed power away from centralized governments and placed it in the hands of organizations, multinational corporations, and international regimes, among others" (Finel and Lord, 2002: 2). Technological developments mean that everything can be known, seen, tracked, profiled and used against us. This means that what "happens in Vegas, stays on YouTube," (Qualman, 2014) and it is tempting to think that we are entering the age of total information and perfect clarity.

The promises of digitally driven transparency go beyond calls for more information or democratization. The desire for transparency is a hallmark of our times, hailing back to Enlightenment ideals. Corporate scandals, such as Enron's collapse, the Volkswagen emissions scam, Edwards Snowden's leaks about government surveillance and the extensive tax avoidance systems revealed in the Panama papers all point to the value of shining a light on organizational affairs. As citizens, consumers and publics, we have a "right to know," and this demand is increasingly institutionalized in cultural and political life (Hood and Heald, 2006; Schudson, 2015). The focus on insight and oversight takes the shape of Freedom of Information Acts, extensive reporting and labeling demands in industries and a wide range of other attempts to make information accessible and useful. Digital transformations are intimately tied to these hopes about more and better information as a source of human progress.

As a recipe for progress, the transparency formula goes something like this: If more information is shared, we can see things as they really are, and as a result we will make smarter decisions and behave better. With digital technologies, big data and algorithmic intelligence, we will be able to see, know and govern in better ways. No more hiding, no more bias and no more uncertainty. And as a result of this clarity and insight, people and organizations will behave better.

This equation between transparency and control was expressed most famously by the US judge Louis Brandeis (1913) when he stated that "sunlight is the best disinfectant, and electric light the most efficient policeman." Along these lines, transparency takes the shape of a formula for the governance of individuals, organizations and societies (Hood and Heald, 2006; Fenster, 2015), and a solution to all sorts of societal problems and challenges. However, to others, these same processes raise fears about surveillance and disciplinary control. In particular, spectacular revelations of government-led surveillance schemes have propelled these discussions into the news, political debates and the public domain. Surveillance has become such a central part of social life that terms like "surveillance societies" (Lyon, 2006; Marx, 2016) and "surveillance capitalism" (Zuboff, 2019) have entered contemporary academic and popular vocabularies. Edward Snowden's revelation of surveillance programs set up the US National Security Agency (NSA) – including one with the code name PRISM, set up to collect communication through major internet companies – also played a significant role in these developments. The growing awareness that internet companies and data brokers collect and reuse all sorts of digital traces have highlighted the importance of questions about surveillance, anonymity and privacy. These concerns involve a different understanding of digitally driven transparency as an extension of long-standing hopes about total information and possibilities for unhindered insights into the lives of citizens.

Possibilities for observation are not limited to the state. In particular, digital transformations have enabled citizens and stakeholders to keep an eye on governments and companies, and these developments have given rise to new conceptualizations: it no longer suffices to speak of surveillance along the lines of panoptic metaphors, where one centrally located actor observes a population of prisoners or others. Increasingly, surveillance also takes the shape of what Mathieson (1997) calls synoptic observation, where many observe the few, such as when the public oversees those in charge. As a result, the demarcations between those governing and those being governed are less clear-cut (Hansen and Flyverbom, 2015). Despite these developments, surveillance remains a dominant issue in the broader debates about digital transformations and transparency.

In some accounts, the key concern is how increased clarity creates unintended opportunities for strategic disclosure of certain forms of information, secrecy and opacity in some areas. Such perspectives challenge prevalent assumptions about transparency as a direct path to surveillance or accountability and stress "how late modernity creates blind spots, invisibility and therefore to some extent less accountability" (Zyglidopoulos and Fleming, 2011: 703). Transparency, then, becomes a new kind of guise for manipulation or distraction. As Leonardi, Stohl and Stohl (2016) suggest, the contemporary obsession with transparency allows organizations to both disclose masses of information *and* hide in plain sight. For instance, dumping lots of information or disclosing selected materials can be an effective way to create peace and space for a given organization to pursue activities that it may not wish to make public. Information, paradoxically, can be a useful tool if you want to distract people's attention.

While drawing on these different insights, this book sets out to show that there is more to digitally driven transparency than the end of secrecy, the growth of surveillance or opportunities for selective and strategic disclosure. Or put in more blunt terms: it sets out to show that the promises of digital transparency formula do not hold up. We will not have access to perfect or total information. We will not be able to see things as they really are. We will not have technologies that give us all the answers. And people, organizations and societies will continue to have secrets and show what they want, despite technological promises about full disclosure.

FROM WINDOWS TO PRISMS

As a repertoire for understanding transparency, glass metaphors are useful. When organizations decide or are forced to be transparent, we tend to think of it as a simple matter of opening a window on reality, allowing us to see what happens inside and make our own judgment about what is revealed. Glass metaphors, however, also remind us that transparency efforts, like windows, not only let light in – they are also forms of decoration that can be used to showcase something, or to shield us from the world outside. One of the important tricks used by department stores is to showcase products behind glass at night, so that customers have to return during opening hours to touch and try the product on. Also, windows can be shut or opened as we please, and they offer protection from intruders. Finally, glass does not simply or only let light pass through unchanged, but may refract and reconfigure whatever passes through or is framed. Glass with polished surfaces, such as prisms, are particularly prone to refract and change what enters into something else. With digital transformations, such refractions become more widespread and worth exploring, hence the title of this book.

Along the same lines, Gabriel (2005: 22) reminds us of the variety of effects that glass may have:

> Glass is a hard and fragile medium, providing an invisible barrier that allows the insider to see outside and the outsider to see inside. ... [I]t is also a distorting medium that reflects and refracts light, creating illusions and false images. Looking into glass, it is sometimes easy to mistake your own reflection for an image facing from behind. Finally, glass is a framing medium – its mere presence, as in the case of Damien Hirst's famous artistic displays, defines what lies behind it as something worthy of attention, protection and admiration.

This discussion of the complex effects of glass is a useful analogy when it comes to problematizing laudatory accounts of transparency. Those who trust in transparency measures tend to consider information as a direct form of access to social phenomena and processes. But what if the relationship between information and reality is more complex? And what if more information also allows for more opacity or leads to new forms of misconduct?

At its core, the conceptual shift that this book makes is to challenge the metaphorical understanding of transparency as *windows* being opened on reality, and to exchange it for an understanding of transparency projects as *prisms* that create extensive and manifold reconfigurations. The prism metaphor offers a more dynamic and nuanced conception of transparency as a matter of creating refractions and a growing need for the management of visibilities.

To develop this conceptualization of transparency, we also need to probe the underlying views of communication and representation at work in the transparency formula. The link between disclosing information and creating insight is not direct or clear-cut. Windows, open offices and corporate reports only give access to selected or filtered parts of organizations. Leaked files by the millions require extensive sorting and editing before they become useful, and videos, like all other kinds of documentation, require interpretation and contexts to be meaningful. The problem is that most transparency projects are seen as unmediated. We expect them to provide direct, immediate access, and show us things as they really are, but it is not that simple. As Frissen (2017: 15) reminds us "it is often suggested that transparency requires no form of mediation or representation whatsoever. When directness is total, facts are assumed to not only to speak for themselves but actually exist in an objective sense." Most theories of transparency, particularly in political science and business and public administration, rely on surprisingly simplistic and old-fashioned views of transparency as a matter of transmitting information from a sender to a receiver. Such conduit models of communication overlook a range of complications, including power differences between senders and receivers, how mediating technologies afford and shape communication, and a host of complexities related to meaning-making and interpretation (Christensen and Cheney, 2015; Fenster, 2015). Along similar lines, most work on transparency considers reality and representations to be the same. But representations, such as transparency efforts, are never a simple mirror of reality. Despite social constructivists' enduring efforts to establish that objects and representations are not the same – *ceci n'est pas une pipe*, but a picture of a pipe, as Magritte's famous painting reminds us – transparency initiatives still preserve the ideal that we can see things as they really are. But transparency projects provide representations, rather than presentations (Frissen, 2017: 16), and they constitute people, processes and objects in particular ways, and must be understood as performative (Albu and Flyverbom, 2016). This argument points to the generative capacities (Rubio and Baert, 2012) of transparency as a force in the reconfiguration of social realities and relations. Furthermore, it paves the way for dynamic conception of transparency as a sociopolitical phenomenon intimately tied to power (Flyverbom, Hansen and Christensen, 2015), and reminds us that we cannot make sense of transparency without giving attention to the devices, mediations and processes of knowledge production involved (Hansen and Flyverbom, 2015). Such questions have recently become a component of what we can think of as critical transparency studies (Birchall, 2015), which this book also seeks to contribute to. Such approaches pave the way for more inquisitive accounts of transparency and a focus on dynamics of visibility management. Rather than simply associate control with surveillance and transparency with empowerment, they help us recognize the complex relations between processes of seeing, knowing and governing as they enter and are refracted in digital prisms and spaces.

The key concept of this book, *managed visibilities*, suggests that when we disclose something, it is always a managed and mediated process. The resulting insights are rather refractions and manifold visibilities than direct observation, pure insight or full clarity. Reconceptualizing transparency along these lines – as a matter of refracting and managing visibilities – allows us to move beyond transmission views and Enlightenment ideals of full disclosure to understand the complications and mediations at play when individuals, organizations and societies become entangled with transparency efforts. Also, this approach stresses that digital technologies are not transparency machines – they do not simply transmit information or create clarity. Rather, they are social and material forces that contribute to refractions and needs for the management of visibilities. This alternative to predominant conceptualizations of digital transparency offers a novel vocabulary that may help us make sense of what happens when transparency becomes an individual, organizational and societal concern. The conceptualization of visibility management brings into play a range of fundamental human activities having to do with seeing, knowing and governing, and brings together issues normally pursued under disconnected headings such as surveillance, secrecy, openness, transparency and leaks. At the same time, this approach speaks to a more extensive challenge, namely to explore and understand what Walters (2012: 52) terms the "new *territories* of power" associated with "the entanglement of the digital, the informational and the governmental." By focusing on the management of visibilities, this book seeks to rethink and explore the workings of digital transformations and the effects of transparency efforts in the lives of individuals, organizations and societies.

VISIBILITIES AND POWER

There is an intimate relationship between what you *see*, what you *know* and what you *control*. Just think of how the invention of the microscope paved the way for modern medicine and the treatment of diseases. It was not until we were able to observe viruses and bacteria that we could understand these phenomena and start to develop ways of acting on them. Or consider how the emergence of maps made it possible to see, know and conquer new parts of the world. Like earlier inventions, digital transformations fundamentally alter how we make things visible, knowable and possible to control. We can think of many such examples of intersections between material objects, possibilities for insight and a sense of control. Buildings exude invitation and candidness through glass facades and open layouts that signal the end of hierarchy and new possibilities for engagement and oversight. Companies craft extensive reports and disclose information to show that they are accessible and accountable. When WikiLeaks published a flood of classified documents on its web site, the goal was to give us direct access to the secrets and hidden workings of governments. And when cities are plastered with surveillance cameras, it is because they promise to show us what happens in the street and make crime prevention and control more effective. In such accounts, it seems increasingly obvious that digital transformations make it possible to see more and see clearer. The excitement about these possibilities for transparency mainly revolves around questions about quality and quantity – that we have more information, better data, and thus perfect clarity. Similarly, when critical voices speak out against secrecy, it is often with a call for more and better information. Dominant approaches also have a primary focus on observation as a one-way, asymmetric process. That is, who watches who, and what is available to the observer, but not the observed? Such understandings of transparency shape both public and academic concerns about managers watching their employees, principals observing agents or a state carrying out surveillance of its citizens. The issue is mainly to show the asymmetrical and one-directional relations at work in such situations. This focus is an important starting point, but ignores a number of complications at work when information gets disclosed. The situation is not simply that we are under constant surveillance or controlled by an invisible watchdog as depicted in Foucault's famous account of the prison layout, the Panopticon, where inmates never saw their guards, but still acted as if they were monitored all the time. What we have are much more dynamic and complex flows of digital information that increasingly make up our reality.

Many discussions about digital transformations and transparency ignore a wealth of social and technological dynamics, and the concept of managed visibilities seeks to highlights these dynamics. It suggests that the intricate processes involved in producing, circulating, selecting and making sense of information should be our main concern.

To sum up: some tell us that we live in an age of unprecedented transparency and openness where the power of the internet and the wealth of digital data will eliminate secrecy and decentralize power (Finel and Lord, 2002). Others warn us that these "new weapons of mass detection" (Zuboff, 2014) or "weapons of math destruction" (O'Neill, 2016) not only allow for blanket forms of surveillance, but also new forms of inequality and injustice. However, we must think of such sweeping diagnoses of the relation between digital technologies and societal affairs in terms of a much more fundamental concern that this book seeks to unfold. That is, how do digital technologies make us see and know in particular ways, and how do these shape the way we govern and order social affairs?

MANAGING VISIBILITIES

The focus on these relations between technologies, visibilities and ordering frames the investigation of a range of dynamics related to observation, knowledge production, organizational processes and regulatory efforts in the digital domain. The primary ambition is to conceptualize digital transformations in terms of visibility management, and use this conceptualization to articulate how dynamics of seeing and knowing made possible by digital technologies shape a variety of human, material, organizational and regulatory arrangements. To understand these developments, we need analytical vocabularies that help us articulate the workings and implications of digital transformations. Dynamics of visibility are at the center of this investigation and conceptualization. If we want to grasp the role of digital technologies in organizational and political developments, we need to first understand how they produce particular visibilities and permit certain kinds of knowledge production and governance. Digital transformations involve not only technologies that allow for new forms of observation, so that we can see into work processes, organizational activities and so on. The emergence of big data analytics means that the world can be visualized and accounted for in news ways. Such forms of observation do not simply produce transparency, but much more complex and paradoxical visibility practices and forms of social ordering.

The choice of the term *managed visibilities* – rather than transparency, clarity, disclosure, openness or related alternatives – is motivated by a wish to foreground mediated, strategic and dynamic attempts to govern through vision and observation. In many accounts, openness is perceived as a characteristic or feature of an entity, such as an organization. In contrast, transparency is a more relational phenomenon, which, for instance, requires an interpreter, somebody who can process information and make sense of what is disclosed (Etzioni, 2010; Hood and Heald, 2006). Conceptualizations of transparency may point to more relational intersections between information and governance. However, as noted above, the focus is often on the quality and quantity of information and how effectively information is transmitted. The conceptualization of visibility management that I propose is more sociological and focused on the paradoxes and dynamics at play. Whereas more narrow understandings consider transparency to be a matter of ensuring accountability through the timely and public disclosure of information (Schneiberg and Bartley, 2008), this book seeks to conceptualize how all visibility practices reconfigure, rather than represent, objects and subjects. Also, it offers a more nuanced view of digital transformations than the one underpinning transparency studies, and problematizes the assumption that more information creates clarity and better conduct.

Dynamics of visibility and invisibility deserve more scholarly attention. These include the dynamics and tensions involved in the production of transparency, surveillance, opacity and secrecy in the digital age, but also complex relations between objects and their representation in data crunches and other digital formats. Engaging insights from organizational communication, political science and communication theory, the book explores the entanglement of digital transformations and the forms of seeing, knowing and governing at play in the management of visibilities. Unlike most accounts that either celebrate transparency and openness or condemn opacity and surveillance, I seek to disentangle what may be understood as an intricate conglomerate or family of forms, norms and functions of managing visibilities in a datafied world.

THE URGENCY OF VISIBILITY MANAGEMENT

Digital transformations fundamentally alter the way we produce, circulate and make sense of information, how our attention is guided, and how we go about the steering of social affairs. As a result, managing visibilities is one of the key challenges of our times. By exploring the workings and implications of the management of visibilities in different realms – the lives of individuals, organizational processes and societal developments – we get a more nuanced and comprehensive grasp of how digital transformations reconfigure the way we see, know and govern.

The internet promised to give us all a voice, to make information easily available and to create a level playing field for processes of democratization and participation. While hopes about digital transformations are still alive and digital spaces continue to deliver such opportunities, we are also increasingly aware of other consequences of digital transformations. The most obvious of these have to do with surveillance, threats to privacy and the multiple ways in which digital technologies facilitate crimes and illicit activities, but there are also less spectacular dynamics worth exploring. Increasingly, a small number of powerful, private companies are installing platforms and infrastructures that perform important social functions. We access information via Google, we build and maintain friendships via Facebook, assess the value and quality of services and products through online reviews, we buy and sell stuff via Amazon and eBay, and we gain access to cultural products via Netflix and Spotify. As these platforms become the fabric of our lives, organizations and societies they have significant consequences for how we act, think and order social relations. As more and more parts of social life rely on digital technologies and data, their architecture, the values they embody and the roles they play in social and cultural transformations become more important to consider. What kinds of societies, publics and politics are they part and parcel of? And what kind of power do they exert as backbones for the production of knowledge, our cultural memory and the way we craft social relations? These are questions about the roles and responsibilities of digital platforms, and about the role they play in societal affairs. Also, they require multiple kinds of answers and reflections. What this book suggests is that digital transformations can be understood as forces that shape how we manage visibilities and guide attention. To set up this argument, it challenges the contemporary excitement about transparency as a solution to all sorts of problems. But transparency projects have lots of complications, unintended consequences and paradoxical effects, and to grasp these we need to think and talk differently about transparency. At the same time, digital transformations, including digitalization and datafication, condition the pursuit of transparency in significant ways and fundamentally reconfigure how we see, know and govern the world. In response to these issues, the suggestion is that we need to think differently about transparency: as a matter of managing visibilities. What this concept means and implies, and why it is relevant for studies of transparency across personal, organizational and societal contexts is what this book sets out to articulate.

1   Digital and Datafied Spaces

Promises of technological progress have always intrigued humankind. Throughout history, people have imagined what they could accomplish with stronger tools, faster machines and more advanced technologies. Such hopes about technological transformations continue to shape most domains of life, from economies and production over social relations to politics and knowledge. The hopes associated with contemporary digital transformations are no exception. The internet and mobile technologies make it easier than ever to find information and communicate. Big data gives us direct, precise insights into all aspects of human life. Right around the corner, artificial intelligence may lead to faster and smarter decision-making. While we often experience that the reality of such developments is more complicated, most technological revolutions are welcomed with the same kind of enthusiasm (Marvin, 1988). Likewise, many companies and other organizations scramble to stay up to speed and fear falling behind the pace of technology while they are busy attending to the core of their work. As a result, most organizations contain departments and people who are on completely different pages when it comes to understanding and working with digital transformations. That is, organizations are simultaneously doing some things in very handheld ways, relying on digital technologies for a wide range of activities and experimenting with big data or artificial intelligence in some parts. At the same time, governments and policy makers are struggling to keep up with pace of technological innovations, and may be more measured in their responses than most others. But the importance of digital technologies for social and economic developments and a growing focus on data collection and privacy concerns have made digital transformations a salient and visible issue in the news and in global politics. This means not only widespread discussions and negotiations over the meaning and ramifications of the digital revolution, but also the emergence of new institutional arrangements and regulatory initiatives addressing this issue area.

This chapter outlines the nature and shape of the technological environments we presently inhabit. This mapping creates the foundation for conceptual reflections on the ubiquity and centrality of digital technologies and data in the lives of individuals, organizations and societies. These reflections are an important stepping stone for the investigation of how digital transformations make us manage visibilities – see, know and govern social affairs – in new ways.

CYBERSPACE AND BEYOND

The ubiquity of digital technologies and data is increasingly natural to us. Still, our ways of talking about these developments are not very precise. We rarely reflect critically on terms such as the internet, digital technologies and cyberspace, but our ways of thinking and talking about technological transformations have consequences for how we engage and live with them. For long, scholars and others have referred to digital developments as cyberspace or simply the Internet. However, these terms are problematic. The term *cyberspace* makes us think of it as separate and independent from social life. Cyberspace is out there, not in here. It is different from "real" life, and has its own rules and dynamics. We can trace this conceptualization of cyberspace back to early discussions about the relationship between real and virtual words. In particular, early advocates and developers of networked computers saw a need to warn against state interference and other attempts to tame cyberspace by applying existing rules and norms to this new domain (Mueller, 2004). Most famously, Barlow's "A Declaration of the Independence of Cyberspace" published in 1996, sought to cast this domain as different, separate and independent: "Governments of the Industrial World, you weary giants of flesh and steel, I come from Cyberspace, the new home of Mind. On behalf of the future, I ask you of the past to leave us alone. You are not welcome among us. You have no sovereignty where we gather." At the time, these distinctions between different worlds and spaces may have seemed necessary and important. In subtle ways, these vocabularies also served to highlight how cyberspace differed from normal life. Digital spaces offer liberation, networking and engagement, in contrast to the oppressive, hierarchical and excluding nature of traditional social spaces. Such descriptions of digital domains as different continue to come up. In 2000, President Clinton stressed that regulating the internet was like "pinning Jell-O to the wall" because this space was out of reach, not like the rest of our world and more or less ungovernable (Clinton, 2000). Similarly, US President Trump repeatedly speaks of the frightening forces populating "cyber" and stresses the need to take control of this threatening space. Cyberspace, it seems, is the Wild West of our times, a place where things roam wild, and which requires that we develop new types of intelligence gathering, new weapons and new rules of engagement.

Another issue is the widespread use of the term "the Internet" – in singular, capital form – as a shorthand for a wide range of digital developments. A number of things happen when we describe digital developments using this term. We conflate a wide range of technologies, practices and transformations into a singular thing. Also, we focus our attention on technology rather than its uses or societal roles, such as when people state – in awe or horror – that the internet has changed, say, politics, or disrupted an industry. As Morozov (2014) has argued, the problem is that we conflate too many issues, developments and arguments in discussions of the Internet – a catchall term that becomes an obstacle to actual analysis and critical thinking. In the same vein, Ford (2003) points out that "The metaphor of cyberspace simplifies decision making by allowing us to ignore much of the technical and normative complexity of this new set of technologies and social practices" (Ford, 2003: 154). Just like it would seem puzzling to talk about the Electricity or the Railway, it may be time to decapitalize the internet, and maybe even to leave the term behind. As technological innovations become integrated into our daily lives we need to stop thinking of them as separate and grandiose.

The problems with terms such as cyberspace and the Internet are also articulated by Ford in his aptly titled chapter "Against Cyberspace" (Ford, 2003). As he puts it: "There is a tendency to describe the Internet as something more than a sophisticated medium of communication – as instead an almost supernatural discovery. In this discourse – the discourse of cyberspace – each computer is a portal to an undiscovered country; online communications and transactions take place in a digitally conjured parallel domain, an e-elsewhere" (Ford, 2003: 148). Such accounts cast the internet as a separate, autonomous domain. The effect is that we either treat it as outside the reach of normal procedures and forms of regulation, i.e. as a wild west that cannot be controlled. Or that we attempt to normalize it by extending our standards and regulatory frameworks to this space. As Hofmann, Katzenbach and Gollatz (2016: 2) put it, much of the early literature was about the "governability" of the internet: about how to tame this space that seemed outside the reach of centralized, hierarchical political control, and about how to fit the internet into existing forms of regulation and state-driven governance frameworks.

It no longer makes sense to distinguish between cyberspace and the real world (Ford, 2003: 149) – they are one and the same space. In a similar manner, Isin and Ruppert (2015) remind us that we are already always online through multiple devices, such as phones, wearables and internet-connected objects. This ubiquity makes the distinction between online and offline and the description of cyberspace as a separate, virtual domain problematic.

DIGITAL, DATAFIED BACKBONES

Despite their critique, neither Ford nor Isin and Ruppert offer an alternative conceptualization that takes us beyond a capitalized Internet and ideas about a separate, independent cyberspace. But this is what we need if we want a more nuanced and extensive understanding of how digital transformations shape the way we see, know and govern. A vocabulary that highlights the ubiquity of digital and datafied processes needs to focus on the foundational role technologies play in social life. The concept of infrastructures best captures how digital technologies underpin economic, social and political processes. It suggests that we can no longer consider digital technologies to be simple *tools* that organizations and societies can choose to rely on, but must see them as *backbones* that condition human action in very far-reaching ways. This approach also takes us beyond the long-standing focus on contrasting and comparing analog and digital technologies and their respective consequences. The concept of infrastructures acknowledges the centrality and ubiquity of digital technologies, and reminds us that these are real and physical, not virtual. By infrastructures, we normally mean large-scale physical constructions of central importance to societies, such as electrical grids, railways and bridges. Just like we would not consider the railway or other types of societal infrastructure to be separate and independent spheres, we have to see digital technologies as a fundamental component of societies.

However, digital and datafied infrastructures are also different from other ones. Bridges and electrical grids are important, but also largely static things that do little more than allow us to cross water conveniently or turn on the light. In contrast, digital infrastructures do much more than simply transport messages across distance. Such infrastructures consist of multiple digital platforms, different ways of sourcing and aggregating data, and advanced algorithms and visualization techniques. They produce data, not just once or in a form that evaporates. Rather, they keep producing resources – in a form that can be easily copied, stored and reused. This makes digital infrastructures very different from other ones. They can do so many things that a bridge cannot. This also raises the bar on our need to think carefully about what we put into them – the norms and decisions that become built in and come to shape what is possible down the road.

BUILDING DIGITAL INFRASTRUCTURES

Switching on the light in our homes, catching a train or sending an email are so simple to do and we rarely think about what makes them possible. Technologies lay the foundation for many parts of human action and many societal transformations. Just think of the importance of electricity for social, organizational and cultural life. The rollout of electricity to individual households and remote areas was fundamental to the forms and standards of living we now take for granted. With electric light, it became possible to stay up at night and work without being limited by sunshine or less stable sources of light. Electrical engines allowed for the automation of multiple processes, and access to electricity made modern forms of production possible.

Societies rely on extensive and well-functioning infrastructures and technologies, including electrical grids, railways and technological platforms like the internet. These are largely out of sight and taken for granted. We often focus on the comfort, price and speed of the train ride, or on the contents of the messages and other information we send or receive, and care little about the backbones that make all this possible. Such infrastructures are important because they make some forms of action possible and constrain others. They are not neutral or given, but the result of multiple decisions and negotiations about what is important and what is not. In the early days of the railways, each nation had its own gauge width, which made it impossible for railway cars to cross borders (Briggs and Burke, 2002). As a result, cargo had to be unloaded and transferred to a new carriage multiple times on a trip across Europe. Obviously, with the emergence of shared standards for gauges, such nuisances disappeared. These and similar decisions about standardization and the shape of infrastructures are perhaps most evident at the moments where these decisions and valuations are made, because once they are in place, we take them for granted.

DIGITALIZATION AND DATAFICATION

The emergence of digital technologies and media has had similar importance for social and organizational life. The growing ubiquity of digital technologies is evident, and PCs, smart phones and other increasingly powerful and compact devices have become a priority for anyone with the necessary financial resources. Organizations invest substantial resources in digital technology and most governments have e-strategies of various sorts and consider digital technologies as central to the optimization and development of society. The internet is foundational to the developments that this book explores. It has made speedier and more extensive interactions of many sorts possible. These transformations were initially about doing existing activities in smarter, automated ways. Sharing content, communicating and keeping track of things is just plain easier and cheaper via digital platforms. By extension, it is obvious that the internet has widespread consequences for economic, cultural, political and social activities. The need to advance and protect crucial digital infrastructures is as obvious now as it was with electricity and other technological developments in the past.

By *digitalization*, I mean processes whereby analog objects and activities are turned into digital forms. Such examples include newspapers in digital format, or music made available as digital files. These developments have been long underway, and in 1956 a hard disk containing 5MBs storage space – about the size of one song in decent quality – weighed a ton and was hardly portable or affordable. The ability to turn many kinds of activities and information into digital form, such as scanning a painting or turning the songs on a vinyl record into a digital file, are important and in many ways revolutionary. These changes in form make transportation, distribution and copying considerably more affordable and easy.

The definition of digitalization as a matter of converting and distributing objects into digital form is important because it allows us to highlight what is different about what we can think of as *datafication* (Mayer-Schönberger and Cukier, 2014). These two phenomena are not the same. With datafication, multiple parts of social life take the shape of digital data. These activities differ from their analog counterparts, because they leave traces that can be stored, put together and reused in many different contexts. But they also take us beyond digitalization, because the need to transform information or objects into digital form disappears – in datafied settings, they are already digital. Like other technological developments, the current surge in the availability and processing capacity when it comes to digital data is important. Social media searches, phones, internet traffic and many objects all produce a wealth of digital traces that can be compiled, analyzed and used to inform decisions. *Big data* is the term that made such processes of data aggregation and visualization popular and understandable outside IT management circles. Also, the Snowden revelations of mass surveillance schemes and Facebook's Cambridge Analytica scandal have contributed to a general awareness of how our digital traces can be used by others and without our knowledge or consent.

Digital technologies and digital data are woven into the fabric of social life. We hardly notice any more, but most of our activities are increasingly digital and datafied. Buying a common product, such as a refrigerator, involves a number of digital platforms and will leave an extensive stream of digital traces. As to the first, our search for a suitable product will quickly take us through search engines, rating and review pages, and price comparison sites. All of these rely on digital technologies that make the circulation, aggregation and reuse of digital data possible. By the time we decide on a brand and model, we trigger yet another chain of digital events, activating warehouses, sales units and delivery companies. Before all this happened, the sourcing of components and construction of the product involved a wide range of digital transactions, just like many parts of it are likely to contain chips that leave multiple digital traces throughout their travels and assembly processes. The fridge still cools our food and looks roughly the same as when it became a common household item 100 years ago. But everything around its production and trade has been transformed radically by digital developments and all parts of our engagement with the item produce a long and dense exhaust of data.

As Zuboff (1985; 1988) suggested long before the present hype about big data and data-driven strategies, digital transformations allow us to not only automate, but also "informate." By this she means that digital traces and other outputs produced by technologies create novel possibilities for making sense of processes and gaining new insights. If we realize the value of such data, digital technologies can become a resource for organizations and others seeking to develop human capacities and improvements. As suggested by Zuboff (1985; 1988), most digitalization projects still take the shape of attempts to automate existing processes, and to replace humans with machines. Today, more than 30 years later, these kinds of digital transformations – turning handheld processes into automated ones – make up the bulk of what states, corporations and organizations seek to achieve by investing in technology. This is a shame, Zuboff (1985: 18) suggested, since automation focuses on "smart machines" at the expense of "smart people," and leads mainly to the "depletion of skills." If digital technologies are mainly used to automate, "human capacities for teaching and learning, criticism, and insight" are lost, she points out.

Datafication is important because it produces a massive and malleable stream of digital traces that can be a valuable resource in decision-making processes and knowledge production. These developments already shape multiple parts of social life. The main argument of this book is more specific, namely that developments in digital technologies and widespread datafication open up novel issues related to visibility – how we see, know and govern things. If the emergence of the internet was central to the information society, the current dominance of large tech companies and the growth in digital data shape what we may think of as information circulation and information control. This raises important questions about the inner operations of digital infrastructures. An understanding of the workings and operations of digital infrastructures is central when seeking to articulate how visibilities are managed and our attention is guided in digital and datafied spaces (Flyverbom and Murray, 2018).

DATA SORTING PRACTICES

Internet companies and social media platforms focus on compiling and extracting value from user data, and use them to map and target very intimate parts of our lives. To understand how this happens, we need to look at what happens inside digital and datafied infrastructures.

Datafication and the reliance on digital infrastructures involve a wide range of activities that often go unnoticed. Discussions of big data often revolve around the large-scale transformations that people fear or hope for. Data is the new oil, a raw material that will revolutionize economies and business operations, some tell us enthusiastically (Vanian, 2016). Likewise, the reliance on data will solve long-standing problems such as human bias and the limits of science, because "good data beats opinion" (Toonders, 2014). Or as a Google policy director told me, datafication makes it possible to base policies on "data rather than emotions." Similar hopes about the value of data-based insights have been expressed more boldly by *WIRED* editor Chris Anderson. In 2008, he suggested that data could be the "end of theory" because we will have all the answers from data speaking for itself. Others stress that datafication and the reliance on algorithms will have far-reaching consequences because "algorithmic cultures" (Galloway, 2006) will take over the "traditional work of culture: the sorting, classifying, and hierarchizing of people, places, objects and ideas" (Striphas, 2015). And some warn us about the possible pitfalls of relying on digital traces and automated, algorithmic processes because they ignore human experience (Kallinikos, 2013), produce segregation in the shape of "filter bubbles" (Pariser, 2011) and may undermine politics and democracy (Morozov, 2014).

But these grandiose discussions about the societal consequences of datafication take place at the expense of a deeper understanding of the actual processes of analysis and knowledge production involved

(Flyverbom and Madsen, 2015). That is, we have to account for the "little" analytical operations (Amoore and Piotukh, 2015), ways of organizing data (Alaimo and Kallinikos, 2017; Flyverbom and Murray, 2018) and infrastructural arrangements (Easterling, 2015) that underpin and condition digital and datafied knowledge production. Such practices of sorting and structuring digital traces are often overlooked or hard to grasp, but they are central if we want to articulate the ramifications of datafication. The term *sorting* is important here, because it captures the essence of what I am suggesting. Data analysis involves multiple steps, procedures and decisions that can be separated analytically. This unpacking of the work that goes into the production of data-based knowledge is an important addition to exiting considerations about datafication. By sorting, I mean processes of compilation and ordering carried out by humans and technologies. These insights draw from science and technology studies, which have for long insisted on the assembled and fragile nature of all kinds of social phenomena and the work of collecting and sorting that go into the production of all sorts of knowledge (Latour, 1988; 2005; Hackett et al., 2008). Sorting processes can be understood as the steps and procedures involved in the making of big data analyses. For instance, data projects involve a wide range of analytical operations, such as the *production of data sources*, the *aggregation of diverse forms of data*, the *alignment between data and commercial, organizational or societal objectives* and the *visualization of data* for purposes of understandability (see Flyverbom and Madsen, 2016 and Madsen et al., 2016 for more elaborate accounts). I think of these as analytical concepts that make the work that goes into data projects understandable. The attention to sorting processes allows us not only to reflect on the work that goes into the production of these kinds of analyses, but also to consider the worldviews and rationalities involved. Knowledge production always starts from particular ways of thinking about the world, is driven by certain aspirations and holds assumptions about human action. If we seek to make the world around us knowable through qualitative methods and situated modes of analysis – for instance by observing or interviewing – particular features come to the fore. What will be considered in such forms of knowledge production are mainly issues such as human experience, appearance and narratives. In contrast, quantitative and statistical approaches will start from different points of departure – such as numbers or rankings – and have little interest in other aspects. Similarly, data-based analyses rely on particular resources and involve particular kinds of, often automated, analysis and visualization (Hansen and Flyverbom, 2015).

All forms of knowledge production also involve ways of managing visibilities. Different modes of analysis are not merely a matter of choosing one set of tools over the other, but that the world around comes to appear differently as a result of what we look for and take in. If we extend this suggestion to digital and datafied contexts, we realize that only some parts of social life are "algorithmically recognizable" (Gillespie, 2017a) and possible to grasp through data analytics. The point is not simply that only people who are using digital technologies leave traces that can be used for analysis, but rather also that big data analyses start from particular criteria about relevance, focus their attention on some aspects rather than others and rely on technologies with particular affordances.

CRUCIAL MOMENTS AND DECISIONS

Situating processes of digitalization and datafication historically and in relation to social transformations is important because we face a "constitutional moment" (Mueller, 2004) in the making of digital infrastructures, and the decisions we make at present will shape the future. This is why it is important to consider carefully and critically how digital infrastructures – the networks, algorithms and data-sharing platforms that are in the process of becoming natural to us – are designed and institutionalized. Large internet corporations such as Google, Amazon and Facebook have taken on roles as entry points for many uses of digital spaces, and increasingly shape the way we work. They offer a wide range of efficient tools

and services, often at no or little cost to individual users and organizations selling services or products. Through these offerings,
internet companies are building a position as the primary infrastructures and gateways in the digital domain. At the same time, they are
harvesting data, building insights and commercializing these on
a scale that no others can match. Histories of technology are full of
such accounts of moments when crucial decisions about technological formats and standards have been made, and they remind us that
once decisions are made, they are very difficult to alter.
Technological infrastructures become invisible and almost
untouchable. The values, norms and design choices we accept or
decide on will become natural and long lasting, and they could be
different. Seemingly, technical standards and decisions matter. One
telling example is how the original idea about hypertexts would
have created a very different internet if it had not been sidelined
early on by a less ambitious system – the world wide web – consisting of URLs and links. In this system, texts and other objects are
linked in digital spaces – the web – but we can only jump from one to
the other. We may see the same piece of text or a piece of data in
different places, but we do not know where they come from or where
they go as links can be easily be cut by copying and pasting. Ted
Nelson, an early internet developer, had an alternative vision for
linking objects in digital spaces that we have almost forgotten about.
This system, termed Xanadu, would create permanent and visible
two-way links between digital objects and their original producer,
and allow us to maintain the connection between digital objects and
their origins. If we could keep track of a given piece of data, many of
the issues related to property rights and invisible, commercial uses
of data would look very different. Royalties for data could be paid,
and we would not need Google to organize information for us
because the system would always keep information organized,
accessible and visible (Hern, 2014; Lanier, 2014). At present, we
see similar ideas about embedding information permanently in digital objects, such as block chain technologies, which can be used to

embed permanent and verified information in products and records of various sorts.

The more general point is that the history of humankind can hardly be understood without attention to the role of technology and infrastructures, and that our ways of thinking about and dealing with these have wide-reaching consequences.

This chapter has offered an overview of contemporary digital transformations and then highlighted how digital technologies shape the way we collect, circulate and make sense of information. Digital traces from multiple sources allow for new ways of producing knowledge and recognizing patterns (Mayer-Schönberger and Cukier, 2014; Hansen and Flyverbom, 2015). Such messy, real-time correlations constitute a particular, yet subtle, form of ordering that shapes how problems and opportunities are made visible, knowable and thus governable. Articulating how digital technologies are woven into social fabrics offers an inroad into a more nuanced investigation of the social and political consequences of digital transformations. Having articulated how this book conceives of digital technologies, we can shift our attention to the effects of digital and datafied infrastructures for the management of individual, organizational and societal visibilities.

2 Transparency and Managed Visibilities

Media and other technologies make new forms of human action possible, and they do so not only as devices of information, but also as "agencies of order" (Peters, 2015). Such ordering effects are well described and well theorized in existing research on the societal consequences of media and digital technologies. What is less pronounced is that digital transformations have consequences for how our attention is guided, both as individuals and as organizations and societies. That is, they make us see, know and govern in new ways, and shape what we think of as reality. To explore these issues, it may be useful to return to insights from earlier thinking that articulated the relationship between media and human realities and how mediations shape social life. At the advent of modern journalism and news media, Lippmann (1922) reminded us that media put "pictures in our heads." Such pictures condition how humans act on the world, and to study the power of media, Lippmann suggested, we need to articulate how such special interests come to control our view of the world (Turner, 2014). These issues are still salient today, where new types of corporations are taking up roles that are comparable to those of media conglomerates of the past. Not only are tech companies taking over large parts of social infrastructures and becoming the primary spaces for social interaction and entry points for news and other societally important forms of information. Our times are also marked by a growing reliance on largely opaque and automated forms of editing and sorting that require us to both reignite and rethink discussions about the power of media and information. Much like newspaper editors of the past, algorithms select and curate information in ways that have social and cultural ramifications (Gillespie, 2014). Algorithms and digital platforms also set conditions for what gets recognized and highlighted; that is, "they encode the terms by which a given cultural production can even be recognized by the social and technical systems that have deployed the algorithms" (Turner, 2014: 253). Whether as engines of distribution or sorters of information, digital technologies are centrally involved in the shaping of how we see, know and govern the world around us.

If we want to grasp the role of digital technologies in organizational and political developments, a focus on how they produce visibilities and facilitate social ordering is central. The argument about the intimate link between seeing, knowing and governing has important conceptual foundations in the work of Foucault and later contributions (Foucault, 1969; 1988; Shapiro, 2013; Brighenti, 2007). Such work also paves the way for the argument that practices of seeing and knowing constitute the foundations for organizing, governing and ordering social affairs. This conceptual and analytical approach allows me to connect issues about observation (seeing), knowledge production (knowing) and societal and regulatory formations (governing) around a focus on the management of visibilities and the guidance of attention. This is important because digital and datafied infrastructures have ordering effects by producing visibilities and guiding attention – i.e. they shape how we make things visible or invisible, knowable or unknowable and governable or ungovernable. This analytical framework is useful if we want to identify dynamics and developments related to the consequences of digital transformations in social settings.

NEW ANALYTICAL VOCABULARIES

Digital developments seem to produce as much fear as excitement. To some, we live in an age of total information where basic, established principles associated with democracy and human rights are under threat by digital transformations. Such approaches focus on questions about surveillance and exploitation: who is tracking me and abusing my privacy, who owns my data and how do we ensure the protection of basic rights in this area (Andrews, 2011; Tranberg and Hasselbach,

2016). At the other end of the spectrum, we have widespread excitement about data as the path to societal optimization, where all problems can be solved through better technologies and perfect information. Driven by Silicon Valley-style dreams about "artificial intelligence" (Russell and Norvig, 2010), "singularity" (Kurzweil, 2006) and the "end of theory" (Anderson, 2008), such approaches start from and end with technology, and have little focus on social, ethical and political concerns.

The problem with these accounts are not just the obvious one, namely that they ignore nuances and tend to misrepresent what technologies may and can do in social contexts. The problem is also that they tend to rely on explanations and lines of argument that belong to a relatively narrow set of registers. For instance, critical approaches to technology often take the shape of justice-based and ethics-oriented arguments about freedom, privacy and human rights. That is, we need better protection against surveillance, tracking and business monopolies in the digital domain, and more opportunities for participation, transparency and voice. In contrast, more excited approaches tend to focus on technological and economic potentials, and largely disregard the importance of political, social and cultural contexts. However, neither dystopian nor utopian registers exhaust what we need to consider when it comes to digital transformations.

We do not yet have the necessary vocabularies to fully articulate the effects of digital transformations for individuals, organizations and societies and the subtle forms of power and control at work. My suggestion is that one addition should be a conceptual language that captures how digital technologies make us see, know and govern social worlds in novel ways. As Zuboff (2019) puts it, internet companies are increasingly in "the reality business" – they collect, extract value from and approach us via our life worlds and come to shape what we value and recognize as important (Gillespie, 2014). Tech companies do not simply mine data, but also our realities and private lives for product optimization, behavioral modification and other commercial purposes. Extending this idea along the lines of the focus on visibility management, it is important to keep in mind that digital infrastructures also shape how we understand the world around us. That puts internet companies in the reality business in a dual sense – as both miners and editors of human realities. These developments raise fundamental questions about representations and realities. They also take us beyond the present focus on individual companies, the workings of digital platforms and the opacity of algorithmic operations, and require new conceptual explorations.

The shift in orientation and register that I propose in this book is to make questions about visibility, transparency and information control more central in our discussions of digital transformations. The emergence of seemingly total information, the excitement about the big data revolution and concerns over blanket forms of surveillance and data aggregation, such as those carried out by the NSA, point to these fundamental issues about the sorts of visibilities that are produced and managed in the digital age. But they are far from exhaustive, and often fall back on simplified registers, as we have discussed. Vision, information and knowledge are central aspects of power and deserve more scrutiny, particularly in the age of big data, autonomic computing and radical transparency. Also, we need analytical vocabularies that invite us to engage more deeply with questions raised by developments in digital technologies, data crunching and the role of information and knowledge production in governance. Visibilities and the guidance of attention are fundamental dimensions of the ordering effects of digital technology, and we need to add them to the list of consequences we normally associate with digital technologies, such as economic developments, democratic transformations and rights issues.

SEEING, KNOWING AND GOVERNING

To appreciate the importance of a focus on visibilities, we need a particular conception of how digital transformations shape social worlds. As digital technologies become ubiquitous and infrastructural, we have to shift our attention to the more subtle and intricate ways they shape our possibilities for action and order social worlds. Digital technologies are so ingrained in communicative practices and organizational and social life that we need accounts that focus on practices, interactions and visibilities. To this end, a distinction between regulation and ordering is useful (Hofmann, Katzenbach and Gollatz, 2016). If we understand the governance of social affairs primarily as a matter of deliberate, institutionalized and formal attempts at *regulation*, we miss the more subtle ways in which human actors and material objects come to shape the conduct of others, that is, contribute to processes of *ordering*. As Gabriel (2015: 17) puts it, such forms of control are "far subtler, yet deeper . . . pervasive and invasive" and do not "merely constrain a person but define a person." It is increasingly through digital technologies that we come to know the world around us, make ourselves visible and are seen by others. Such activities are intimately connected to power and control. Digital infrastructures and processes of datafication have power effects because they shape what we see and know, and because these visibilities come to guide our attention. My argument is that if we want to understand contemporary digital transformations, we need to start from these questions about visibilities and their relations to power and ordering. With a focus on how individuals, organizations and societies manage visibilities, we can capture how digital transformations allow us to curate our presence and guide the attention of others in fundamental, yet largely unnoticed ways. By *manage*, I mean not how a manager seeks to regulate the actions of his or her employees, but much more encompassing processes of ordering or the steering of conduct. So, the management of visibilities is about how digital infrastructures and datafication allow us to act on the world through what we can see, know and govern (Flyverbom et al., 2016).

The argument that seeing, knowing and governing are intimately connected is both seductively simple and dreadfully intricate. It is obvious and unsurprising that it is only when we can *see* things are they *knowable* to us, and only then that can we *act* on them. To see, know and govern our surroundings is something we do all the time: Responsible individuals regularly look at their bank account, understand that they are spending more than they earn and start adjusting their behavior so the deficit does not grow further. Organizations report on their activities to make them visible, so that regulatory bodies of various sorts can know what they earn, how much they pollute or what they are importing, and regulate and govern them accordingly.

However, the historical and conceptual trajectory of the idea that seeing, knowing and governing are inseparable phenomena is long and meandering. Modern science rests on such assumptions and so does the Enlightenment ideal about rationalization and human progress. Philosophies and sociologies of knowledge, visual sociology, work on the politics of knowledge and the literature on transparency, surveillance and secrecy all hinge on these questions in one way or another. In the context of my argument about the relationship between seeing, knowing and governing as a way to understand visibility management in digital spaces, the primary source of these ideas is the work of Foucault and extensions of his writings on knowledge and power. The idea that practices of seeing, knowing and governing are intimately connected is central to Foucault's work on governmentality and the many later contributions that have extended his ideas into just about all parts of social science (Foucault, 1979; 1988; Dean, 1999). While Foucauldian scholarship focuses mainly on the importance of language and discourses, the extension to visibilities is relatively unproblematic. An overview of these ideas and their permutations is outside the scope of this book, and can be found elsewhere, such as Brighenti's (2007; 2010) ambitious and thorough work on visibility as a category and key concern in sociology. Rather, the point is that these contributions lay the foundation for the conceptualization of managed visibilities and the guidance of attention in this book. What Foucault – in what often comes across as convoluted and scattered writings – helped us grasp was that forms of ordering always revolve around particular ways of seeing and perceiving, involve distinctive ways of thinking and questioning and work through concrete practical rationalities and techniques of intervention (Foucault, 1988; Dean, 1999). These issues take us beyond the well-known example of the Panopticon, a prison designed to manage visibilities among prisoners and guards in ways that maximized inmates' sense of being observed and minimized the need for guards to observe inmates. Digital transformations afford a much wider range of visibility practices and ways of governing through visibilities. Managing visibilities is always also a matter of regularizing particular kinds of conduct and categorizing and positioning people, i.e. a matter of power: "Who [can] see what, whom, when, where, and how ... remains an integral dimension of the everyday operation and experience of power" (Otter, 2008: 1). Similarly, Brighenti (2010: 148) suggests that "The management of visibilities lies at the core of all forms of social control, whether formal or informal. More precisely ... control consists of a purposeful and contextual asymmetrisation and hierarchisation of visibilities." Extending such ideas into broader processes of social ordering is a valuable starting point for the study of visibility management in a datafied world.

Digital technologies are central to the proliferation of extended and novel forms of observation and logics of surveillance. As a result, Foucault's panoptic model of centralized surveillance and self-discipline (Foucault, 1977) no longer stands alone, and we see the emergence of other forms of observation and control, such as synoptic ones where the many watch the few (Lyon, 2006).

Also, it is important to keep in mind that the same cameras, in the streets or on the bodies of police officers, can be used for panoptic and synoptic forms of observation. The purpose of such cameras may be for authorities (the few) to observe citizens (the many), but in the process, citizens (the many) also get opportunities to observe how authorities (the few) handle their roles and treat citizens. Digital technologies, such as body cams, mobile phones and wearables give individuals a wealth of opportunities to record and publish their interactions with police officers and other authorities. These developments are also captured in work on "sousveillance" (Mann et al.,

2003; Ganesh, 2016), describing situations where the "few watch those in authority from below." Such digital possibilities for multi-directional forms of observation add to the complexity and importance of visibility management as an empirical and conceptual concern.

Taken together, these issues can help articulate how digital technologies and visibility dynamics generate novel ways of seeing, knowing, organizing and governing human affairs. At the same time, they can add texture to the argument that a focus on the management of visibilities gives us an enhanced understanding of contemporary digital transformations. But an approach focusing on how visibilities are managed involves a rather different understanding of transparency, and one that requires a bit of unpacking.

FROM TRANSPARENCY TO VISIBILITIES

The theoretical backdrop to this book is an exciting body of scholarly literature on transparency. Such accounts include attempts to make sense of the role of information sharing in both close-knit and more distant social relations (Etzioni, 2010), and a wealth of discussions about the potentials of "sunlight" to work as a "disinfectant" (Brandeis, 1913) in such different fields as anti-corruption, regulation, management and organization. As articulated in my introductory discussion of the "transparency formula," most accounts focus on how information is disclosed in the name of transparency, and assumes that more information will lead to more clarity and better conduct. The main questions are then whether the disclosed information is plentiful and encompassing enough, whether it is good information or not, and whether it is the right information being disclosed. The emphasis on these three dimensions of information – quantity, quality and relevance – is obviously reasonable and important. This focus on features of information is also an important starting point for what most people and organizations expect from transparency efforts: that we get good, plentiful and relevant information about the inner workings of an entity that helps us verify that it really is and does what it promises. Along these lines of thinking, a good transparency project is one that involves symmetrical information flows and does not keep one party in the dark (Brin, 1998). Most scholarly and public discussions of transparency fall in this category and have a focus on transparency as a matter of verification through information disclosure (Albu and Flyverbom, 2016). Such information-focused approaches not only imply a particular conceptualization of transparency as information, measured in terms of quality, quantity and relevance, they also have a primary focus on the conditions that make transparency projects possible and efficient, and measure success in terms of how information makes people and organizations act responsibly (Brin, 1998; Schnackenberg and Tomlinson, 2014). But there is a much more foundational issue to consider, and this is the understanding of communication that underpins such approaches. As suggested by Fenster (2015), the underlying theory of communication at play in most transparency research is a "transmission" approach, where questions about efficiency, the minimization of noise and related transmission issues are central. That is, transparency is understood in terms of simple conduit (Axley, 1984): a sender compiles or produces information and transmits it via a given channel to a receiver, who may react with some feedback or other kinds of responses. Such views of communication as transmission processes typically assume that recipients have the necessary skills and literacies, that channels of communication are neutral and stable and that messages are not affected by the surrounding environments and human interpretations (Fenster, 2015; Christensen and Cheney, 2015). For organizations, this means that as long as they disclose good and plentiful information about their inner workings in a manner that is understandable to those around it, we would not have to worry about misconduct, secrecy and other maladies associated with closed books. Also, such research makes a sharp distinction between transparency and secrecy. In such accounts, digital technologies are largely considered conduits for transparency. As Greenberg (2012) put at it the height of excitement about WikiLeaks and related whistle-blower and transparency projects, digital technology is a "machine that kills secrecy."

However, recent research has suggested that transparency is not simply a digitally facilitated process of transmitting information that gives more clarity and results in better conduct. Transparency efforts, like other forms of communication, are full of complications, ambiguities and other forces that the "transparency formula" and transmission approaches do not capture. This is why this book suggests a communication perspective – a focus on complex processes of meaning-making and interpretation – as an important entry point for understanding transparency and its consequences. By conceptualizing transparency as a communication phenomenon, we move beyond the focus on information simply being transmitted, and start to consider the complex communicative, organizational and social processes involved in attempts to make something transparent (Hansen and Flyverbom, 2015; Albu and Flyverbom, 2016). Such approaches also highlight difference, paradoxes and negotiations, and challenge the assumption that more information has positive effects on human conduct. Transparency projects, like other forms of communication, are often strategically ambiguous (Eisenberg, 1984) to accommodate different understandings and aspirations. As Weick and Browning (1986: 254) remind us, "Vagueness is a source of power, a form of slack, and a means of building consensus," and these are the sorts of dynamics that a communication approach attunes us to. Finally, with a communication approach, we become more open to the idea that transparency efforts do not merely reproduce or mirror a reality "out there," but become important forces in the making or reconfiguration of realities and understandings of objects and subjects (Flyverbom and Reinecke, 2017). Or put differently, transparency projects do not merely verify something pre-existing, but also play a performative role in the making of social worlds.

Historically, all sorts of transparency projects and other kinds forms of visibility management are inseparable from technologies and techniques in use. Obvious examples include censuses and other ways in which states seek to make populations legible for purposes of governance (Scott, 1998), or more recent ambitions to use big data techniques to develop a "social credit system" that rates and ranks Chinese citizens based on their digital footprints (Botsman, 2017). Other examples include corporations' uses of ICTs to make work practices visible (Zuboff, 1988) or when information-gathering and -circulation comes to shape multiple social domains (Gleick, 2011). But the point of this book is that visibility deserves a more central place in our conceptualization of digital transformations. Managing visibilities and guiding our attention are such fundamental features and uses of digital technologies that they shape all other activities and possible effects of digital transformations. Conceptualizing transparency as part of a broader complex of digital transformations that condition new forms of visibility management is an important step in my attempt to articulate that technologies are not simply machines that "kill secrecy" – rather they afford processes of seeing, knowing and governing.

MANAGING VISIBILITIES AS KEY CONCEPT

We can think of visibility management as a foundational, social phenomenon. We all show some parts of ourselves and keep others private, and navigating in social contexts requires a sense of what to disclose and what to conceal. As suggested by Goffman (1959), social interactions always involve "frontstages" and "backstages," and humans display themselves carefully and strategically in different contexts and in the face of social expectations. The concept of visibility management extends this understanding of human action into broader organizational and social process in digital and datafied contexts. This extension relies on important work seeking to establish visibility as a general category in sociological thinking. Drawing together insights from a wide range of areas, Brighenti (2007) ambitiously develops visibility as a "sufficiently general descriptive and interpretive social scientific category" that may enhance and nuance our understanding of a range of social phenomena. This book extends such efforts by exploring how our understanding of digital transformations can be enhanced and nuanced if we conceptualize them in terms of transparency and the management of visibility. Obviously, a range of more classical sociological categories and concepts could be used to unpack current developments in the area of digital technologies, and we now have a vast literature discussing digital developments in terms of systems, actors and networks. But the point of this book is to show that concepts and explorations of transparency and visibility offer new and valuable insights into key developments in the digital domain.

Insights from the literature on affordances also feed into my argument. As I have suggested with colleagues, we can think of visibility as a "root affordance" (Flyverbom, Leonardi et al., 2016) that allows for the branching of other affordances, such as the ability to store and edit information or form relationships through information (Treem and Leonardi, 2012). This implies that the horizon of possibilities offered by digital technologies is anchored around processes of visibility management, and that other affordances emanate from visibility, making it a central force in the shaping of organizational and social life. As a technological affordance and social force, visibility is not only fundamental, but also encompassing. By this I mean that it must be understood as an umbrella concept for a range of visibility practices. Secrecy, transparency, surveillance, opacity and leaks are not separate phenomena, but part of a family of concepts and practices with significant resemblances (Hansen, Christensen and Flyverbom, 2015). Existing accounts of the digital domain and the sociopolitical effects of information technology mostly treat these as separate phenomena, and often consider transparency to be "simply the opposite of secrecy" (Coombs and Holladay, 2013: 217), or distinguish sharply between (good) transparency and (bad) surveillance. In contrast, a focus on visibilities offers a more encompassing approach that articulates their shared dynamics and entanglements. As later chapters in this book show, secrecy and transparency are inseparable in organizational settings, and a sharp distinction between the two is problematic, both empirically and politically (Birchall, 2015; Costas and Grey, 2016). It is much more productive to approach transparency, secrecy, opacity, leaks and others disclosure practices as members of a family of concepts related to processes of vision and observation (Garsten and de Montoya, 2008; Hansen et al., 2015).

A comprehensive analysis of how visibilities contribute to social ordering therefore requires that we look at the intersections between transparency and other visibility practices. The investigation of how transparency intersects with other visibility practices and recipes for how to govern social affairs through disclosure is important because it brings out the tensions and paradoxes of transparency. The focus on entanglements and families of visibility practices suggests that transparency resembles other "impure practices that have mutated as they become mobile across time and space, and increasingly complex as they have articulated with other logics and forms of rule" (Higgins and Larner, 2010: 215–216). Also, the focus on intersections between different visibility practices offers new conceptual and empirical avenues that we need to explore and navigate in times marked by ubiquitous digitalization and datafication. Such attention to entanglements across different visibility practices at work helps us address important dynamics and power effects that digital transformations come with.

DYNAMICS OF VISIBILITY PRACTICES

These dynamics of visibility management are multiple, and an outline of the most important ones is a useful starting point for both empirical and conceptual explorations.

Visibilities and Performative Dynamics

Transparency and other visibility practices must be understood as generative dynamics of seeing, knowing and governing, and this conceptualization differs markedly from predominant approaches. If we consider transparency as a matter of making information available, the primary issue is how much of it we can have and digest, whether it is good or bad information and if it is delivered in a timely manner and when we need it (Rawlins, 2009; Fung, 2013). While such concerns about the amount, inclusiveness and quality of information being disclosed are certainly important, they also guide our attention away from more fundamental questions about the conditions and contexts that shape disclosure and information control. Also, they distract from the more complex task of understanding the ways in which information comes to perform particular functions that have little to do with its size, quality and timeliness. To engage with these questions, there are valuable insights from the literature on performativity (Austin, 1962) that can help us make sense of transparency as a dynamic phenomenon that "works back upon those subject to it in ways that are often counter productive, or at least far exceeds the passive image of a simple making visible" (Roberts, 2009: 958). That is, transparency is not a simple matter of reporting on or disclosing information about an already existing phenomenon – it also brings into being the objects and subjects that it seeks to make transparent. If we think of transparency as performative along these lines, we are better equipped to understand it as a social process and a phenomenon with generative capacities (Rubio and Baert, 2012). This has implications not only for how we conceptualize transparency as a form of communication and meaning making, rather than transmission of information, but also for our understanding of its functions in processes of social ordering. In particular, it points to the need to move beyond the view of transparency as a matter of observational control, such as in principal-agent models, and toward a more refined understanding of transparency as a form of productive power that creates distinctions, boundaries and relations (Flyverbom, Christensen and Hansen, 2015). That is, transparency ideals and practices do not only work as extensions of control or solutions to problems of power, but must be understood as sources of power and control in and off themselves. Transparency efforts are ambiguous forms of control – "diffuse and relational, constituted in interaction and mobilized in discourse" (Flyverbom, Christensen and Hansen, 2015) – that contribute to the constitution of subjects, the production and stabilization of meaning and other forms of ordering (Clegg and Haugaard, 2009; Flyverbom, 2015). This understanding of visibility management as performative is an important first dimension.

Visibilities and Directionalities

Discussions about transparency often focus on how to increase amounts of information. This focus is limiting, because "it narrows the analysis to the question of more or less transparency when the real question concerns the directions and varieties of transparency" (Heald 2006: 34). A directional conception of transparency is better attuned to the idea that transparency projects may open up new zones of (in)visibility in and around organizations. The focus on directions of transparency, such as inward, outward, upward, downward (Hood and Heald, 2006) is an important stepping stone, even if it tends to reproduce assumptions about principals and agents somewhat uncritically and give little attention to processes of interpretations and negotiation.

This approach is in line with the suggestion to focus on constellations of concepts such as panoptic, synoptic and other forms of observation, and the call for a family-resemblance approach (Haugaard, 2010; Hansen et al., 2015). This allows us to integrate multiple forms of vision and disclosure, such as secrecy, opacity and transparency, under a shared focus on visibility management. Taken together, these discussions pave the way for a more dynamic conception of transparency that this book seeks to offer. To conceptualize these patterns, we can rely on Heald's (2006) distinction between different "directions of transparency." Heald (2006) makes a distinction between the directions transparency can take, and on the varieties of transparency that exist. Transparency can either be directed upward or downward, in the sense that the hierarchically superior can observe the conduct of subordinate, or the ruled can observe their rulers. In horizontal terms, transparency may be directed outward or inward, as when an agent can observe what it happening outside the organization, or when those outside can observe what is going on inside the organization. Where outward transparency and inward transparency coexist, there is symmetrical horizontal transparency (Heald 2006: 29). This conceptualization not only suggests that information flows in different directions, but also that transparency can be symmetrical, so that all parties in principle have access to the same amounts of information about each other (Heald, 2006: 26–29). But to appreciate the workings of transparency as a form of ordering, we need an even more elaborate understanding of the dynamics involved. Transparency efforts can be understood as attempts to act on the world by managing possibilities for seeing, knowing and governing. That is, transparency always involves decisions about what to disclose and to whom, but also questions about flows of information and directions of visibility in concrete settings and projects. By differentiating between upward, downward, inward and outward forms of transparency, and by adding that these forms of transparency are ultimately about the management of visibilities, we are able to see that transparency always involves choices, asymmetries and divisions – who can observe whom, which activities are opened up and which kept closed and which objects and processes are subjected to transparency efforts and which are not?

Other attempts to think about directionalities in observation include discussions about the role of digital technologies in new forms of surveillance and digital possibilities for multi-directional forms of observation. Reflections about such developments are important because they constitute new ways of shaping the "conduct of conduct," and point to the increasingly polycentric nature of governance, where subjects are simultaneously governed and governing, and where visibility becomes a central feature. A dynamic conception of visibility management and its workings in the context of governance needs to pay attention to the multi-directional and polycentric nature of vision and observation in the digital age.

Dynamics of Interpretation, Translation and Meaning-Making

It follows from this that we need to pay much more attention to the situated and practical workings of vision and observation, because it is here that the "generative capacities" (Rubio and Baert, 2012) of such activities may produce particular (in)visibilities. One entry point for such understandings of the practical workings of visibility management is to focus on the meanings given to transparency and related ideals and practices. By placing emphasis on processes of communication, interpretation and meaning-making, we can appreciate the many ways in which transparency projects imply more than making information available (Tsoukas, 1997; Roberts, 2009). Transparency is best understood as an ambiguous, partial and impermanent "script" (Sahlin-Andersson, 1996) that is circulated, edited and translated. By implication, transparency is not a unified project or established set of guidelines, but rather a matter of interpretation, editing and association in concrete settings. The central question is how particular actors make sense of, negotiate and engage with transparency ideals and practices in attempts to shape organizational, technical and political formations. In particular, the attention to meaning also invites us to focus on the contexts and situated norms that transparency efforts encounter (O'Neill, 2006). Ideals and practices related to transparency are moving targets shaped by ongoing interpretations and enactments by organizations, legislators, regulators and other stakeholders, and these configurations are central if we want to understand how visibility management relates to social ordering.

Taken together, these dynamics substantiate the suggestion that transparency and other visibility practices are performative, and have organizing properties that contribute significantly to processes of social ordering. Transparency projects and other visibility practices are not simply tools that we can use to mirror, verify or illuminate a world out there through information. Rather, they are forms of ordering that produce individual, organizational and social realities (Roberts, 2009;

Albu and Flyverbom, 2016). Transparency projects are performative in a number of ways. They are *normative* and *disciplinary* in the sense that they set standards for conduct and operate as forms of either direct control or more invisible forms of regularizing power (Flyverbom, Christensen and Hansen, 2015). Transparency efforts also perform important roles when it comes to *recognizing* and *identifying*, because it is through disclosure that people, organizations and other actors are seen and have their stories told (Brighenti, 2010). Furthermore, transparency projects are *asymmetric* and *strategic*. They create visibilities as well as invisibilities, and always emanate from somewhere – politically, ideologically and in other ways. These performative dimensions are central to my suggestion that visibilities constitute a central organizing and ordering force in a datafied world. Managing visibilities is a form of social ordering that produces relations and boundaries. This is also why a focus on managing visibilities and processes of seeing, knowing and governing is an important entry point for studies of power and control in times of digital transformation. This analytical framework focusing on performativity, meanings and directionalities operationalizes the argument that visibility is intimately connected to efforts to see, know and govern, and serves to guide the analyses and empirical illustrations in later chapters of this book.

INSIGHTS AND REFRACTIONS

Drawing on insights from sociologies of visibility, media and internet studies and the transparency literature, this chapter challenges the view of transparency as a privileged and direct mode of seeing, knowing and governing. This problematization of information- and transmission-oriented approaches to transparency paves the way for a more disenchanted and dynamic conceptualization of transparency as a form of visibility management. Managing visibilities is a fundamental, social phenomenon and involves complex communication processes. Along these lines, the chapter argues that digital technologies do not produce transparency in the sense of simple reflections or direct observations, but rather create refractions and reconfigurations. The metaphor of a digital prism is a starting point for novel ways of studying the dynamics of visibilities and transparency in processes of governance in the digital domain. Such avenues for research focus on the generative capacities of visibility practices, and pay attention to directionalities, meaning-making and entanglements as central features of visibility management.

The focus on how visibilities are mediated and managed has a number of benefits. As an umbrella for a family of concepts, such as transparency, secrecy, leaks, surveillance and opacity, it invites us to explore intersections among different visibility practices and to highlight their shared dynamics.

At the core, these are questions about information control: how we as individuals, organizations and societies handle, circulate and visualize information of various sorts. But questions about information control are rarely addressed – or only in a piecemeal fashion – by sociologists, political scientists and organization and communication scholars. This may be so because the disclosure of information may seem like a technical or innocent matter. We deliver a report, publish a set of numbers or share visual documentation like a photograph, and tend to take them for granted as representations of a given situation or phenomenon. But, obviously, we could have written something else in our report, the numbers could be read differently and the picture could have been taken from another angle. Whoever we shared this information with would see something different. That is, the visibilities we produce could have been managed differently. These banal reflections serve two purposes: first, they remind us that information control and visibility management are foundational, social phenomena, and central to human, organizational and societal conduct. But digital transformations have intensified possibilities for visibility management, and created the need for reflections about this phenomenon. This is also stressed by Shapiro in his discussion of visualization, which he describes as "the proliferation of techniques of picturing, showing, reproducing, and displaying the actual, the artificial, and the fantastic" (Shapiro, 2013: 1–2). Information control and visibility management also have analytical value. That is, they invite us to think about a range of practices in new ways. This implies that much of what we normally understand and describe using other vocabularies, such as work, routines, identity formation, and editing, can be studied in terms of managed visibilities and forms of information control.

3 People under Scrutiny

Our personal lives are shaped by digital transformations in very obvious and tangible ways. Billions of people spend hours a day sharing, commenting and liking photos and stories. We have easier and better access to all kinds of information, and more and more daily activities take place in digital spaces. Most people coordinate their work and social relations in new ways, and many use digital technologies to raise awareness of what they do and who they are. Digital technologies make communicating, sharing and engaging with others easier than ever before. These developments blur the lines between what is public and what is private, and require that we reflect on what openness and privacy imply in a datafied world. But digital transformations also shape our lives in more fundamental and subtle ways. How we sense and experience, how we depict ourselves and how we understand the world are inseparable from digital technologies and the environments they give rise to. Digital spaces and data exchanges are increasingly the foundations of our existence, whether we like it or not. At a rapidly growing pace, they offer new possibilities for action and guide our conduct in important ways.

Still, our ways of talking and thinking about these developments are lagging behind. We have spent many decades considering the features and effects of other kinds of resources for thinking and acting, such as narratives or numbers. We recognize the important roles played by our shared stories about the past, anecdotes about good and bad behavior and tales about the forces deciding our fates. These guide human, organizational and societal conduct, and we have articulated and precise vocabularies to rely on when we discuss their importance (Ricœur, 1990; Czarniawska, 1998). Similarly, we have a solid grasp of how numbers and statistics shape social life. We divide cities into postal codes. We count populations for purposes of governance. And we make decisions about uncertainties based on statistical probabilities. Numbers are an important resource for our wish to see, know and govern the world, and we have a strong body of research and a well-developed sense of how numbers guide our conduct as individuals, organizations and societies (Hacking, 1990; Desrosières, 1998). By comparison, we have only started to grapple with the question of how digital traces, automated forms of processing and data visualizations affect the way we live and think. Unlike narratives and numbers, digital data are largely foreign to most of us. Similarly, we may have a good grasp of the work that a statistician, narrator or news editor engages in when sorting through information. But the sorting operations of an algorithm seem less comprehensible to most people. Reading an annual report or making sense of a narrative account also seems more straightforward than interpreting a complex and colorful data visualization.

VISIBILITIES AND INDIVIDUALS

These questions about visibilities and the guidance of human attention are not entirely new, but they do differ from the orientations of most existing research. The proliferation of digital spaces has been matched by a burgeoning literature seeking to make sense of how they shape the lives of individuals. To some, the main issue is how digital technologies affect work and everyday habits. Others are more interested in how we form communities and build social relations in new ways as a result of these digital transformations. For some, questions about identity are central, such as understanding how online and offline selves intersect or differ. To others, the primary concern is how established and emergent rights such as freedom of expression, privacy and security are shaped by digital transformations. Focusing more directly on technologies, important work has articulated the different workings and affordances of technologies when it comes to sharing information and collaborating; for instance, that they allow for continuous editing, make processes visible, enable collaboration and ease the storage of information (Treem and Leonardi, 2013). Scholars have also shown interest in algorithmic operations and their social significance, and there is an exciting literature on the sociology of algorithms in the making (Gillespie, 2014; Striphas, 2015; Cheney-Lippold, 2017). Finally, taking a more rights- and regulation-oriented approach, important discussions about surveillance and privacy have taken center stage in research and public debates about digital transformations (Brunton and Nissenbaum, 2015; Lyon, 2015). Such research continues to articulate what makes digital transformations significant for humans, individually and collectively. But as this book suggests, these developments should also be understood in terms of the visibility practices involved, and the intricate forms of ordering that they give rise to. This is not to say that studies of social formations, identity work or rights issues are somehow flawed or based on faulty assumptions, but simply that an analytical vocabulary focusing on visibilities and processes of seeing, knowing and governing makes it possible to bring out new dimensions and important dynamics of digital transformations. When information and data are produced and circulated via digital technologies, features such as speed, persistence and reusability allow for new ways of observing, sharing and capturing patterns related to human behavior. Also, digital technologies afford novel opportunities for peering into otherwise opaque activities, such as the private communication of citizens or the way people select and value different kinds of information. The result is a growing and interesting tension between peoples' desire to share and open up their lives, and the fear about loss of privacy and discomfort with covert forms of surveillance and corporate demands that we disclose our real identity on digital platforms. All these developments make the management of visibilities a more pressing issue than ever before.

Digital transformations and the visibility dynamics they afford lead to particular forms of conduct. These shifts in behavior are not only about strategic, conscious or purposeful human action, such as what people share, like or comment in digital environments, but also about much more invisible and automated operations by algorithms and other sorting mechanisms that aggregate, recirculate and derive meaning from masses of digital traces. These issues are important to understand in general and will require extensive research in years to come. But they are also urgent from the perspective of individuals here and now. Everything we do in digital spaces is a potential resource for marketing agencies, data brokers and others seeking to understand how we think and behave. Also, more and more people are realizing that digital technologies allow governments and intelligence agencies to peer into their private communication and make otherwise opaque activities intelligible. As a result, we need not only research, but also new kinds of awareness, skills and principles that can guide us through life in digital and datafied worlds. The discussions in this chapter focus on how digital technologies shape the conduct of individuals by creating particular flows of information and dynamics of visibility. It illustrates how digital transformations require people to manage visibilities in new ways, and seeks to articulate some of the literacies, strategies and principled issues involved.

THE TRANSPARENT INDIVIDUAL

The lives of individuals seem to be more observable and public than ever before. Social media platforms are populated by people broadcasting their opinions, meals, bodies and other glimpses of their lives. There is a growing number of applications and devices that promise to give us insights into parts and workings of our bodies that were previously inaccessible – how we sleep, how many steps we take and even how many thrusts our sexual intercourses involve. Such offers to see, know and govern human bodies appeal not only to health-minded individuals, but also corporations seeking to optimize the efficiency of their employees. Many states invest in technological systems that make them able to carry out blanket forms of surveillance and collect a myriad of data points about their citizens and outsiders that pose possible threats. The transparent individual, whose every move can be observed and assessed, is here, it seems. Hollywood productions, such the 2017 movie *The Circle* about a Silicon Valley tech company pursuing full transparency when it comes to employees, work and the world as a whole, and non-fiction titles, such as *I know who you are, and I saw what you did* (Andrews, 2011), also speak to these issues. In response, privacy advocates and others concerned about human rights stress the need to tame the use of digital technologies and protect individuals. But these developments in information sharing, the monitoring of human behavior, surveillance schemes and the increased focus on rights and responsibilities in digital spaces are often discussed without much attention to human activities and coping strategies. So rather than simply state that individuals are becoming transparent, we need to explore how people navigate in and are shaped by digital transformations.

People increasingly have to become managers of their own information and the digital traces they leave. Because information is difficult to control and delete in digital spaces, individuals have to be in charge of their digital presence and history on a continuous basis. And when they fail to do so, the consequences may be dire. News stories about revenge porn, the hacks of personal photo collections and cases of social media posts backfiring on people days or years later all speak to this. As processes of digitalization and datafication become ubiquitous and infrastructural phenomena, individuals not only become targets of extensive forms of profiling, tracking and surveillance, but also deeply involved in the circulation, structuring and management of information and visibilities.

The consequences of these developments can be explored by asking how digital transformations come to guide our attention and our conduct. How are we seen, known and governed through visibilities? Who are observing us? For what purposes? And how do we act differently as a result? It is important to stress that in the context of digital spaces, we are not simply talking about humans managing their visibilities actively and directly, but also about the reality that we are managed and sorted by algorithms in complex and opaque ways. The question is what selections are made on our behalf – what we are served or directed to – when automated and algorithmic modes of visibility management enter social life. At the core of these issues is a relationship between visibilities and *recognition* and *control*, as Brighenti (2007; 2010) has shown in his foundational and important work. Visibilities, he suggests, cut to the core of human existence, and should be a key component of our sociological imagination. Digital transformations only add urgency to this argument. Increasingly, we are made relevant and recognizable through digital technologies and the digital traces we leave. One obvious consequence of these possibilities for increased visibility is that they allow for recognition. We are able to see and acknowledge who people are and what they do, and also seemingly able to unveil peoples' needs and motives. Recognition has been a key concern in discussions of the value and potential of digital technologies. Early discussions about the internet as a source of democratization, expression and dialogue had this focus. Recent work in organizational communication has explored how digital technologies enhance visibility by making people see work processes, the activities of co-workers and information streams in more effective ways (Treem and Leonardi, 2013). But, as Brighenti reminds us, visibility is about much more: "The relationship of looking at each other constitutes the site of mutual recognition, misrecognition or denial of recognition of the other – in short, the site where we constitute ourselves as 'subjects.' Vision is subject-making: something like a 'subject' is born only through the creation and development of the visibility relationship itself" (Brighenti, 2010: 27). The suggestion that visibilities make humans into subjects is an important Foucauldian point, which has mainly been explored under the heading of the Panopticon. The architectural design of a prison where inmates could not know when or whether they were observed by guards, and therefore acted as if they were guarded all the time, obviously illustrates how humans become particular kinds of subjects when observed. But the effects of visibilities are more manifold, and the relationship between observation and control cuts deeper into social affairs. This is why the key concept in this book, managing visibilities, both seeks to offer an umbrella for a range of visibility practices such as surveillance, transparency, leaks, opacity and secrecy, and starts from a focus on the relationship between seeing, knowing and governing. This allows us both to acknowledge how visibility works as a source of recognition and control and how it relates to a host of other dynamics. The main value and contribution of this approach is that it is integrative and analytical, and suggests that we can study how digital transformations shape the lives of individuals in terms of the management of visibilities.

AUTHENTICITY AND ANONYMITY IN DIGITAL SPACES

Questions about who you can be on the internet and the relationship between online and offline personas have been central in a lot of literature on social media and digital transformations (McKenna, 2009). The key concern has been to articulate how new forms of connectivity and social relations are propelled by social media platforms (van Dijck, 2013), and what these developments mean for individuals and their possibilities for expression and engagement.

Over time, we have seen a development from early hopes that the decentralized nature of the internet would allow for anonymity. Because you could seemingly hide behind your screen and pretend to be someone else, the hope was that digital spaces could protect, for instance, vulnerable activists from prosecution, and allow alternative voices to be heard in situations where governments or other actors seek to limit expression. More recently, it has become clear that the internet also allows for the exact opposite: everything you do is stored, tracked and visible, at least to some. These realizations are both the results of spectacular revelations about government surveillance and a growing awareness of data aggregation for commercial purposes. But they are the propelled by a movement toward verified, real identities as a norm in digital spaces. Mark Zuckerberg, for instance, put it this way in an interview: "You have one identity . . . The days of you having a different image for your work friends or co-workers and for the other people you know are probably coming to an end pretty quickly. Having two identities for yourself is an example of a lack of integrity" (Kirkpatrick, 2010: 199). Some people may use different names, birth dates and other inaccurate information, but the goal is to establish as much verifiability and correspondence as possible. The demand for authenticity is described as a way to increase security and trust in digital spaces, but clearly also ties in with need to have reliable data to mine and aggregate for purposes of profiling users and targeting advertisements. Even though platforms may have billions of users, each of them counts: Facebook, for instance, makes $3.82 per global user and $14.34 per user located in the USA each year (Funk, 2016).

As van Dijck (2013: 201) puts it, such platforms have obvious interests in positioning "the online self as a standardized tradable product." If emotions and preferences can be linked to individuals, the resulting data obviously has value for marketing agencies and others segmenting and targeting audiences for commercial purposes. The focus on verifiability also becomes tied to subtle decisions about sorting and valuing information. The demand for real identities is not only pursued at the moment we sign up on digital platforms, but increasingly also when different kinds of information are given value in these spaces. Cohen and Schmidt (2013) suggest that content whose source and other identifiers can be verified will be valued over anonymous information on digital platforms, such as Google. As we all know from searching online, the information that comes first is often what we go with, and anonymity may be one criterion that pushes some content to the bottom of the list. While such decisions may seem reasonable and uncontroversial, they institutionalize particular conceptions of what social arrangements should look like and how human visibilities are valued.

Besides the corporate value of connecting digital traces to identifiable individuals, there is also a growing focus on verified identities as the only way to ensure that people behave properly. Anonymous communication may bring out the worst in some people, and seems directly linked to hate speech and cyber bullying (LaShel, 2012).

Disclosing who you are, on the other hand, creates accountability and better possibilities for social norms about acceptable behavior to be institutionalized. While both anonymous and authenticated forms of presence seem to have benefits, there is an increasing pressure for verification, as well as a growing realization that anonymity is more or less impossible in times of fine-grained data aggregation and the reliance on advanced tools for correlation. Also, it is important to consider the implicit ideas about integrity and consistency that underpin this worldview. As West (2017) reminds us, internet companies consistently cast the demands for authenticity and verifiability in terms of community values and trust, and downplay the link to possibilities for commercial profiling and economic gains.

These developments are part and parcel of the spread of ideals about transparency, authenticity and verification as the foundations of social order in and beyond digital settings. While this drive to show what people and things really are like has ties to Enlightenment ideals and plays out in therapy and court rooms alike, digital transformations seem to give it new momentum. Decisions about what you disclose and considerations about how it is interpreted must take into account that your identity is evident to everyone, and that the reach and permanence of information on digital platforms has few limits (Mayer-Schönberger, 2009; Marwick and Boyd, 2011). Also, as research has shown, not very many digital traces need to be combined in order to identify a person (De Montjoye et al., 2015). In times marked by a growing demand for verifiability and fewer possibilities for anonymity, the ability to manage visibilities becomes more important than ever.

MONITORING OURSELVES AND OTHERS

Technologies like fitness trackers, lightweight cameras and smartphones allow for unprecedented forms of monitoring and information sharing. We can keep track of our exercise and sleep patterns over time and compare with those of others. The work of doctors and police officers is recorded and increasingly made public via digital platforms, and surveillance cameras are a natural part of most cities. These developments have far-reaching consequences that we are only beginning to grasp. Moving beyond the confines of health clinics and consultations with our doctor, our well-being becomes a much more individualized and visible phenomenon, and something that we can engage with in multiple new ways. In combination with advanced and affordable genetic mapping services, such as those provided by 23andMe and similar companies, health monitoring is increasingly popular and easy to do. But the personalization and datafication of health raises difficult questions about private and public boundaries and the consequences of data aggregation and circulation. While comparing your health data with those of your friends may be fun and useful, the same data may be used by your insurance company to calculate your premium or help an employer decide whether or not to hire or promote you. Such worries are not even fictional – for instance, many fitness tracking companies have user agreements that allow them to sell data to data brokers and other third parties and many devices suffer from extensive security weaknesses (Hilts, Parsons and Knockel, 2016). The very possibility that your health and fitness data could end up in the hands of insurance companies, advertisers or employers creates the need for careful visibility management on the part of the individual, as well as better formal regulation and more reasonable and flexible privacy policies. At present, these are rarely the first thing we think about when monitoring our number of steps or hours of sleep, and very few of these companies offer their users guidance on how to deal with these issues.

In contrast, surveillance cameras and body cams are a more obvious form of monitoring, and increasingly part of public discussions about the value of transparency. Streets are equipped with surveillance cameras, police cars have dashboard cams installed and a growing number of police officers are asked to wear body cams. Police departments, particularly in the USA and Europe, promise full transparency and disclosure as a way to handle concerns about police violence and corruption. Adding to such forms of extensive monitoring, many encounters between police officers and the public are caught on cell phones and made public via video sharing platforms like YouTube and live streaming features on social media platforms. This equation between constant monitoring and better police work or public safety is easy to understand, and the main focus seems to be on providing more and better footage and coverage. Here, as in other contexts, more and better information is seen as a direct path to transparency: show us the footage, and we will know exactly what happened. Furthermore, attempts to air reservations about this simple equation are often written off as attempts to hide or distort what actually happened. But it is worth questioning the equation, because increased monitoring is not the direct access to reality that we are promised, and the delivery of transparency through live camera feeds raises a host of problems and unintended consequences that we are only starting to understand.

As to the first point, it is not very surprising that what we see in a recording is not reality or truth, but a selective slice taken from one vantage point. But even if this is a banal observation, we need to keep in mind that cameras and other monitoring devices both condition particular kinds of insight and require interpretation and contextual knowledge that are never part of such recordings (Ready and Young, 2014). Certain details will be more relevant to some audiences than others, and the broader context is rarely caught on camera. As Ready and Young (2014: 5) put it: "Different viewers may contextualize the event differently in terms of how it is framed in their mind, how they think it was precipitated, and what they think happened in the 30 seconds before the camera started rolling. The technology doesn't provide this context – being human does." Videos are also selective and managed forms of visibility that only capture selected parts of what happened in a given situation.

What is more surprising are the unintended consequences and strategies that have to be developed to handle transparency programs relying on dashboard and body cams. Consider the case of the Seattle police force. In 2014, the police department lost a case about the public disclosure of its archived video material in Washington State Supreme Court. The case started when a reporter from a local TV station requested access to video recordings made by Seattle police officers with reference to the Public Records Act, which states that "in the interest of transparency and responsibility to all residents, taxpayers and other constituents' public records can be made available, with very few restrictions" (www.seattle.gov/public-records). The problem with police recordings, however, is both the sheer volume that digital body cams and dashboard cams produce, and the resources it takes to prepare the material for disclosure. The manual process of going through every single frame and redacting sensitive parts of a recording is extremely labor intensive and would be crippling if a lot of requests were made. While the Seattle Police Department had a sense of these potential ramifications of the case when they lost it, it took a zealous individual to show just how impossible promises about transparency can be. Annoyed that the TV station only published snippets of the material it now had access to, a local citizen named Tim Clemans, who states he got into it as a hobby, started filing all sorts of requests for information (Funk, 2016: 34). For instance, he asked for every single video ever recorded by the Seattle Police Department, asked 60 different state agencies for all the emails they had ever sent, and asked the University of Washington to share all its records since "the earth was formed billions of years ago." While some police departments in the state complied, most of his requests were denied because of the difficulties of processing all the information. As one agency noted, it would take 132 years to compile and disclose all its emails (Funk, 2016: 34). The bombardment of requests for these types of information show that transparency is not simply a legal or ethical matter, but also a practical problem. And, as this book will argue again and again, the results of transparency efforts are managed visibilities, not full disclosure. In Seattle, the proposed solution, surprisingly, came from Clemans himself. His suggestion was to develop an automated system that would add a light blur to all police videos requested for public access. While the result is a fuzzy blur, this technique – over-redaction – would make it possible to disclose all videos quickly on public, digital platforms such as YouTube, without having to edit them in line with privacy or security concerns. If particular segments then grabbed the interest of the public or others, they could be processed manually and disclosed. What we get is not transparency, but a blurry, managed visibility that makes it possible to both run a police department and live up to public and legal expectations about transparency and accountability. Still, the result is far from perfect, and many people in the video could easily be identified based on the audio, where names, addresses and other personal details come up. But the example shows that the balance between what to disclose, what to conceal and how to manage visibilities is central to all sorts of transparency projects.

These developments in digital technology and police work have caught the attention of many critics and scholars (Goldsmith, 2010; Meikle, 2016; Newell, 2017), and, as a result, we know more about how they affect privacy, legitimacy and perceptions of police work. Also, these initiatives are part of wider attempts to solve problems related to accountability, trust and legitimacy through what you can think of as observational control (Flyverbom, Christensen and Hansen, 2015). But these are not new questions, and one of the earlier and most interesting discussions about the issue can be found in Marx's book on police surveillance from 1988:

> Powerful new information-gathering technologies are extending ever deeper into the social fabric and to more features of the environment. Like the discovery of the atom or the unconscious, new control techniques surface bits of reality that were previously hidden or didn't contain informational clues. People are in a sense turned inside out, and what was previously invisible or meaningless is made visible and meaningful.
>
> *(Marx, 1988: 206–207)*

Pre-empting many contemporary discussions of surveillance and data aggregation, such discussions of technological transformations are central to the issue of managed visibilities. We have touched upon the issue of digital traces and data packages, and cameras and similar transparency devices feed into the same hope for full disclosure and unhindered insight.

The links between digital transformations, datafication and the care for humans raise many questions about the techniques used to see, know and govern ourselves and others in new ways. I have pointed to cameras and trackers as illustrations. These are all instruments of societal care or self-care in a Foucauldian sense. They are intended to decrease ambiguity about events and actions, help us optimize our lives, and program our future conduct. At the same time, such digital developments blur the distinction between public and private and require considerations about visibility and control because our conduct and possibilities for action are shaped by such transformations.

CURATING OUR DIGITAL DOUBLES

Cultural and social life is increasingly shaped by digital platforms and an abundance of data streams. But we rarely consider what these streams consist of, how they are structured and used and how they make us act in particular ways. Digital traces and algorithms produce what we can think of as our data doubles (Ruppert, 2011): very fine-grained representations of who we are, what we like and where we have been. Increasingly, these data doubles are used by advertising agencies, intelligence analysts and other to segment, profile and track individuals. While such attempts to see, know and govern individuals are not new, it is important to consider how data doubles relate to other forms of knowledge production, such as asking people or accounting for them through numerical representations (Hansen and Flyverbom, 2015). Also, we need to consider the implications of these data sources and algorithmic techniques being largely in the hands of corporate and state actors (Boyd and Crawford, 2012). The growing reliance on digital doubles raises questions about information control and the power at work in managing visibilities, including how these developments shape our view of the world and guide our attention.

One area where these developments have significant conse-quences is hiring processes and job searching. The identification of talent increasingly involves extensive searches and investigations of potential employees. As Berkelaar (2014) points out, such forms of cybervetting not only reconfigure hiring practices, but also put new demands on job seekers. Whereas traditional background searches rely on institutionalized and standardized public records, interviews and peoples' own descriptions of their merits, digital transformations allow for much more extensive, unstructured and extractive forms of exploration. People post photos on social media platforms, appear in news stories, debate in various forums and leave extensive digital footprints that employers may find more revealing than a polished résumé or a generic list of positions and achievements. Because employers look for "applicants aligned with organizational brands, they extend ... work expectations beyond conventional temporal, physical, or fiscal employment boundaries: 'Everything needs to be tight' because 'you're hiring the whole person'" (Berkelaar, 2014: 496). One result of such developments is that all kinds of activities become relevant for work and part of a much more extensive and less control-lable curriculum vitae. From an employer perspective, the underlying rationale is obviously that insights into peoples' *actual* behavior are valuable, especially because it limits the possibility for surprises once the contract has been signed. At the same time, applicants may not be aware of the ways and the extent to which they are scrutinized, and may never find out what information made a potential employer decide against hiring them. Much like immigration authorities, who tend to make decisions about visas and other travel requirements without explanation, employers can make up their mind based on a selection of material that applicants do not have access to nor are able to control fully. When such information becomes the basis for decisions about employing someone, and the person is not given the opportunity to explain or contextualize what comes up, the need for managing visibilities is evident. Cybervetting also transforms our understanding of what is deemed relevant information for hiring decisions, because all kinds of situations and activities potentially become part of the picture. Whether or not such information asymmetries are expected and accepted, or such investigations are seen as a violation of social norms may differ from one setting to another. But certainly, as cybervetting becomes a key component of hiring processes, job seekers must carefully manage the traces they leave and curate their digital presence (Berkelaar, 2014). This is no simple matter, and requires extensive labor – both proactively and reactively. In the end, the responsibility for the management of these visibilities lies with the individual, and even incorrect, false or misleading information becomes part of the digital double that individuals must live with. This individualization of responsibilities is an important consequence of digitalization and datafication. Adding to this, we know little about when and where we produce data, who gets access to them and what operations are involved when they are used as the basis for decisions about us. Regulatory attempts to deal with the consequences of these developments are largely piecemeal and limited in their degree of efficiency. For instance, the European Commission (2012) has passed legislation that promotes the "right to be forgotten": Under this framework, citizens can ask Google to remove content from searches, although the original sources may remain available. So far, Google has removed links to 738,358 sources (Google, 2017). At the same time, we see the emergence of companies offering services to people in need of "online presence management," such as www .reputationdefender.com.

The digitalization and datafication of human lives create situations where managing visibilities becomes intimately tied to career and job planning. Here, as elsewhere, the stakes are high, and the needs for competencies are central. The question is not merely about the responsibilities of individuals when it comes to maintaining a clean digital record, or about how much employers and recruitment agencies tell us about their practices. The most important issue is the novel space for visibility management that opens up. More than ever, we need to consider how our behavior and interactions appear to others when they become digital traces and are reused for other purposes and in different contexts. The constant visibility management for purposes of employability is driven by a seeming acceptance of transparency and possibilities for insight as a natural state of affairs. But we also need to consider that how to make space for anonymity and secrecy – politically, organizationally and in our imagination as humans and employees – and this is a question in need of our sustained attention.

TRACKING, PROFILING AND TARGETING INDIVIDUALS

The consequences of developments in human tracking and profiling are more extensive than most people realize. You may have noticed that the t-shirt you looked at briefly in an online store seems to follow you as you move on to other web sites. Maybe it was not available in your size, and maybe you decided against it for another reason. At any rate, the stickiness and insistence produced by these uses of your digital traces tend to be as annoying as the pop-up ad or other attempts to get your attention. But these are only the dumbest and most visible uses of the digital traces we leave. Some uses are much more effective and unknown to most people. The free personality quizzes that often come up in your Facebook feed are a case in point. Does he really like you? Are you naughty or nice? Who is your soulmate or best friend? If you were an ice cream, what flavor would you be? After a couple of minutes of distraction and a fun post to your friends, you move on. But so does your data and that of hundreds of thousands others. Your responses to the different questions in the quiz, in combination with all your updates, likes and comments, as well as information about all your Facebook friends are now in the hands of whoever offered you the quiz for free. Cambridge Analytica was one of those companies. With the slogan "better audience targeting," the company used Facebook quizzes and other online resources to build very extensive and fine-grained profiles of your personality traits and preferences. The company, like others operating in the same space, boasted that it had around 5,000 data points on more than 220 million people (Cambridge Analytica web site and Funk, 2016b). These were gathered from commercial data, voter data and various digital and other sources. But what is particularly important about these developments is not the sheer volume or extensive coverage, but rather the uses they can be put to. Using advanced digital platforms and more fine-grained profiling, companies like Cambridge Analytica rely on psychological profiles, such as what is known as OCEAN scores (Openness, Conscientiousness, Extraversion, Agreeableness, Neuroticism) to target individuals with so-called "dark posts" that reach only the selected person and are attuned to the exact needs or soft spots of that individual. Such direct targeting makes sense if you want to make somebody act in a particular way, like vote for a candidate, and know enough to be able to focus on that one piece of information that may be decisive. Cambridge Analytica worked for the Trump campaign in the 2016 election, and used these techniques to target messages to very narrowly profiled individuals. As an article in the *New York Times* suggested, such techniques made it possible for Trump campaigners to ensure that "a pro-gun voter whose OCEAN score ranks him high on neuroticism could see storm clouds and a threat: The Democrat wants to take his gun away. A separate pro-gun voter deemed agreeable and introverted may see an ad emphasizing tradition and community values, a father and son hunting together" (Funk, 2016b). Because of the individual and micro-targeted nature of such forms of influence, there is little possibility for alternative viewpoints or debate about the truth value or myopia of the information spread this way. Unlike television ads that require presidential candidates to state that they have paid for (or "approved") a given ad, such forms of direct marketing operate at the edges of or outside the realms of established forms of regulation. Using the same technologies that promised more democratization, dialogue and interaction, such emergent forms of advocacy and profiling open new questions about the operations and regulation of data-driven forms of advertising, campaigning and advocacy. The kinds of managed visibilities that such attempts to influence peoples' mindsets and decisions rely on change the way we have traditionally thought about political debates, the circulation of material and the emergence of collectivities. These tendencies for digital platforms to feed you content from people like yourself have mainly been discussed under the headings of "echo chambers" and "filter bubbles" (Pariser, 2011; Hosanagar, 2016). But the issue is not just that people tend to prefer information that is in line with their own worldviews – in digital spaces and elsewhere – but also that these visibilities are managed in ways that are hard to discern and influence for individuals.

SETTING PRIVACY AND USER CONTROLS

Digital transformations create new types of visibility management in the space between humans and technologies, such as product design, technical solutions for privacy protection and user controls. The emergence of technical and design solutions allowing individuals to control their digital information is particularly widespread among tech companies such as Google and Facebook. In response to growing concerns about the use and abuse of personal data for purposes of profiling and marketing, many digital platforms offer ways for people to manage information. These include privacy settings and dashboard functions giving users an overview of their own posts, their subscriptions, digital histories and various relations with the companies. The most well-known of these are probably Facebook's privacy settings that allow you to decide whether a post should be seen by only your "friends" or made public on the platform. Such settings are presented as ways of providing control and transparency, and intended to enhance trust. As Google's privacy director said at a Senate committee hearing: "As we work to bring more relevant ads to our users, we continually seek to preserve transparency and user control over the information used in our ad system" (Whitten, 2010). Similarly, Facebook has a focus on how to improve users' control over data and what the company terms digital histories. Google has gone further in the attempt to support and institutionalize such initiatives across its various services and products, for instance by setting up what the company referred to as the Data Liberation Front, a team of engineers tasked with making it easier for users to move data in and out of Google products and services. These developments mean a number of things: they offer individuals a number of possibilities for control, but within the confines of digital environments that are already structured with data aggregation in mind. That is, the control a dashboard gives us is not that we can opt out or know what happens to our data, but rather that we can decide who (of our friends and followers) can see or not see particular things. They may even distract people from the fact that everything they do on and through connections with Facebook becomes a resource for the company.

It is rarely possible to grasp exactly how much information about individuals digital platforms actually have. But there are cases such as the Austrian student, Max Schrems, who relied on the European "right to access" provision to make Facebook disclose every single record that the company had on him. What he received from Facebook was a CD containing more than 1,200 pages of data (Hill, 2012), and while extensive, Schrems still claims that Facebook withheld some of his data. Another example is extensive and fine-grained location data. If you use Google services, go to www .google.com/maps/timeline and see how it has tracked and mapped every movement you and your phone have made, at least since 2009. From a business point of view, total information is what digital platforms aspire to, even if their missions and public announcements are cast in different terms, such as sharing, connecting and providing access.

Despite the public focus on the masses of personal data that companies like these have, it still surprises many how varied and rich this information is. As the search optimization company, Wordstream, has visualized, Facebook contains fine-grained information about your locations, gender, age, relationship status, languages, education, work, family relations, political orientation, life events, preferences in music, film, products, food and drinks, your sports activities, the digital devices you use and what you support, like or speak out against. In combination with various kinds of other information obtained through partnerships with data brokers, the result is an extremely fine-grained picture of who you are and what you like and may be developing an interest in. This, obviously, is exactly what advertising companies and others eager to see, know and govern individuals dream of. As a result of news stories and research in this area, we may be aware just how much information such digital platforms have about us. What is less visible is an emergent industry of private data brokers that collect, analyze and package masses of personal data in order to sell customer profiles and market segmentation services. Such companies, operating in a largely invisible part of the marketing industry, include Axciom, whose data packages include extremely fine-grained information about individuals, much like those described above, but put up for sale and packaged in all possible forms. For instance, The World Privacy Forum has documented that such companies can sell you lists of rape victims, people with dementia and HIV or AIDS, or any other segment that you may be interested in knowing more about (Hicken, 2013).

The amount and quality of these masses of personal information and the role they play in commercial transactions are important. But what does navigating in such spaces require from us as citizens, consumers and educators? Largely, digital platforms recast contested political and regulatory issues about privacy and rights as personal matters and individual responsibilities. More than ever, we need to control and curate information if we want to stay in charge of our presence on digital platforms. Rather than a regulatory issue to be solved by policy-makers, privacy becomes a technical matter of managing settings, a corporate promise that we have user control and a set of social expectations that people are able to exercise digital citizenship and responsibility. This is yet another way in which the management of visibilities becomes a key feature of digital transformations and the datafication of everyday life.

One of the consequences of the Snowden revelations is a growing market for encryption software and the proliferation of tools that allow people to move through digital spaces without leaving traces. One such tool is Tor Project, a free software and open network that allows people to be anonymous online. Such tools have been used by activists and criminal groups for long, and the very use of something like Tor may mean that people are seen as suspicious. But there is a growing market for such tools that make it possible to engage in various forms of digital self-defense. As people become aware of the constant and endless ways in which their data can be accessed by others, the use of technological forms of protection becomes more widespread.

Digital transformations entail new forms of visibility management; for instance, in the shape of product designs, technical solutions for privacy protection and user controls. The reliance on material forms of visibility management is particularly prevalent in internet companies such as Google and Facebook. At present, data protection and privacy play a pivotal role in discussions about digital transformations and the business models of internet companies based on data aggregation. We also see emergent regulation focusing on the right to be forgotten, the right to erasure and other ways of dealing with digital traces (Mayer-Schönberger, 2009). But as this chapter shows, such discussions about policies and regulation are often re-cast as technical by the corporations involved. Thus, corporate initiatives to deal with these concerns rely on particular mechanisms for the management of visibility, for instance in the shape of design features allowing users to see and alter the information and data that companies can access and store. But just because users of digital platforms have opportunities to look into products and how their data get shared, these remain limited and curated possibilities for control and customization. The promise that we can control information sounds increasingly hollow as we start to realize that data aggregation and profiling based on our traces are the norm rather than an anomaly. This gulf between individual and state forms of visibility management that we are offered by internet companies is striking, and illustrated most vividly by surveillance efforts that seek to observe citizens and foresee potential dangers without their knowledge. They indicate that digital platforms consider the control with digital traces to be an individual responsibility, rather than something to be regulated by governments or a responsibility that companies should take on. This is why there is a growing need for us to consider how we manage our visibilities in digital spaces.

HUMAN EXPRESSION AND EXPERIENCES

Concerns about the possibilities for human expression and experience through digital technologies have taken very different shapes in the relatively short history of the internet and more recent processes of datafication. While such developments are never clear-cut and linear, we can identify three relatively distinct phases. Early considerations about the internet and the virtual communities (Rheingold, 1993) it made possible had a primary focus on the increase in *choices* for individuals. Rather than have to rely on what government institutions, newspapers with direct ties to political parties or state-funded television stations served up, digital spaces would allow people to access the information they wanted and preferred. With the globalization and commercialization of news and other cultural products, came also more choices and variety for most users. We can think of these possibilities for distribution of content as an increase in our *freedom of choice*, made possible by digital transformations.

With increased opportunities for not only distributing, but also producing content, people came to understand and be excited about digital spaces in new ways. As the internet became available to more people at greater ease and lower costs, the focus shifted to the possibilities for users to generate and distribute content through web sites, blogs, social media platforms and so on. The internet promised to be a new pathway into deliberation, democratization and participation, driven by active and empowered individuals. We can think of this phase as marked by an excitement about digital possibilities for *freedom of expression.* In more recent years, our way of talking and thinking about developments in digital technology seems to be shifting again. As individuals, we enter and are used by digital spaces in uncountable ways. We are profiled and segmented by companies and advertising agencies and targeted with products that we may be prone to buy. We are under surveillance from governments, and whatever digital traces we leave may be used against us. At the same time, we use a range of tools to compile and share information about ourselves, but also to keep other kinds of data to ourselves, for instance by encrypting or hiding information. The trust in digital spaces seems to be in decline, particularly as a result of people's growing awareness of government surveillance, leaks and data breaches and corporate exploitation of our personal data (Flyverbom, 2017). These developments highlight that digital transformations do not only give us more choices or ways to express ourselves, but also raise serious questions about who receives and reuses the data we produce in these spaces. Not only do our digital traces spread and stay in digital spaces in largely uncontrollable ways, but what we say and do is also controlled by whoever owns the platforms and sets the guidelines for what is deemed acceptable and valuable (Gillespie, 2018b). This means that when we upload or share information, we have no way of knowing what happens to it, who receives it and who uses it for what purposes. Only around two-thirds or fewer of our Facebook posts reach our "friends" (Gessler, 2017), and many other sorting decisions and mechanisms are outside our control. This raises questions that go beyond choice and expression, and involves what we may think of as (limits to our) *freedom of reception.* As argued above, the idea of user controls and dashboards in digital platforms is somewhat misleading. When the data we share and produce is seen as valuable for other purposes, we have only limited possibilities for keeping track of them or knowing where they end up. This is why we increasingly worry about what happens to our data in digital spaces, and need to consider not only the production end, but also what takes place inside digital platforms and on the receiving end. These are the questions that the focus on managed visibilities seeks to respond to: how are our data streams controlled, who gets access to what kinds of information and how is human conduct shaped by the resulting visibilities? In different ways, these questions point to a growing importance of visibilities and attention. When information is abundant and easily circulated, getting and guiding peoples' attention becomes central, and managing visibilities becomes a fundamental concern.

The focus on individual visibility management ties in with a wide range of contemporary concerns about the human condition: How can we protect the right to privacy in times of total information and relentless tracking (Mayer-Schönberger, 2009)? How can we master the easy access to information and the wealth of possibilities for storing and reusing data, instead of becoming slaves of technology (Zuboff, 2019)? And what does it mean to be a citizen, a job seeker or a customer in such settings? As this chapter has suggested, digital transformations require that we ask new questions about data, responsibility and human conduct. Often, such discussions about policies and regulation are re-cast as technical by the corporations involved, for instance in the shape of design features allowing users to see and alter the information and data that companies can access and store. But the bigger picture is much more complex.

When information and data are produced and circulated via digital technologies, features such as speed, persistence and reusability allow for new ways of seeing, knowing and governing. At least some of these issues can be addressed under the heading of managing visibilities. These discussions stress how digital transformations shape relations between individuals, corporations and states by creating particular flows of information and dynamics of visibility. The focus on visibilities also invites us to reflect on rights and responsibilities in new ways. Do we consider them to be our individual property, a freely available resource that corporations can extract value from as they like, or do we consider them a type of public good that we benefit from collectively? Questions about visibilities are also ultimately about power and control. That is, how do processes of digitalization and datafication condition particular ways of acting and being? What kind of power relations develop when data becomes a resource for governance? Reflections about these entanglements between visibilities and human conduct are a first step, and one that paves the way for the following explorations of visibilities and digital transformations in organizational settings and societal developments.

4   Organizations Gone Transparent

The excitement about transparency means that many organizations think and talk about their operations and relations in new ways. The public and the press increasingly demand access and insight into the inner lives of organizations, and digital technologies are often seen as disruptive forces that will end secrecy and make it impossible to stay out of sight (Sifry, 2011). The combination of institutionalized transparency ideals and processes of digitalization and datafication is often considered to make organizations more accountable and unable to hide. Such accounts trust in the ability of transparency initiatives to provide direct access to organizational phenomena and processes, often invoking metaphorical images such as "opening a window on reality" and the existence of "naked organizations" (Tapscott and Ticoll, 2003). Also, they stress that those with secrets will need to exercise extreme caution because the mounting pressure to share and open up makes organizations more fluid and accessible.

However, the push for transparency also comes from within organizations. Some companies actively "go transparent" or "default to transparency" by opening up, sharing information and giving access to their insides. Whether driven by outside pressure or inside aspirations, the good organization is largely one that allows for access, insight and involvement, and transparency projects have become one of the hallmarks of organizational legitimacy. Most organizations develop reporting policies and practices, create and respond to expectations about information sharing and install digital systems intended to facilitate communication (Neher, 1997; Neyland, 2007; Studer, 2009). And when organizations disappoint us, the response is often to inspect carefully, turn every stone and insist on confessions. Corporate scandals are an obvious example. When Enron collapsed because of fraud, insider trading and other kinds of misconduct, when Siemens' extensive corruption schemes were exposed and when Volkswagen was caught rigging emissions tests, the first reactions were to call for transparency. To prevent similar forms of misconduct in the future, both the public and policymakers called for more transparency, better disclosure mechanisms and continuous oversight. The irony, of course, is that all these companies were well audited, had a range of disclosure mechanisms in place and published multiple reports and statements on a regular basis. Such situations raise a number of critical questions: Did these companies simply not publish enough information? Could the disclosed information be of the wrong kind, or did they simply select to only share particular kinds of material intended to distract us from their misconduct and to conceal their illicit or unethical activities?

In grappling with these questions, we open up an important aspect of efforts to create observability and transparency in organizational settings. That is, how can we ensure that what is disclosed is the right information, and how should we assess organizational efforts to open up? Largely, research on organizational transparency has also focused on questions about the quality, quantity and relevance of the disclosed material (see Albu and Flyverbom, 2016). We can think of this as information-oriented approaches that focus on transparency as a matter of *verification*. This implies that the purpose of disclosing information is to verify the existence or absence of an object or a state of affairs. It also implies a focus on information as the primary measurement of transparency: the more information we have, the more insight we have. While this may be the case in some situations, we only need to think about phenomena like the info-dumping of thousands of files to distract attention (Stohl, Stohl and Leonardi, 2016) or beautiful big data visualizations that convey little substance or meaning (Halpern, 2014) to realize that just because there is plenty of information, it does not mean that we are able to understand more. Even if the information that gets dumped on us is relevant, we may not be practically or organizationally able to sift through or make sense of it. So thinking about transparency efforts in terms of the quantity, quality or relevance of information is not enough. Or put differently, we need to push beyond the conceptualization of transparency as a matter of information transmission, and think of it as a complex communication phenomenon (Fenster, 2015; Christensen and Cheney, 2015). A distinction between information transmission and communication invites us to consider all the work that goes into producing, circulating and interpreting information and the range of uncertainties and complications involved. It also reminds us that the production of transparency involves both human and technological forms of activity, and different forms of knowledge production (Hansen and Flyverbom, 2015). What is presented as transparency is in fact an ongoing and extremely complex communication process. As Christensen and Cheney (2015: 71) put it, transparency must be defined not as a "precise end state in which everything is clear and apparent, but as *a social value* that stimulates a general quest for information and access." This implies that we need to understand transparency projects as a set of forces and hopes about information as an organizational and societal remedy. Also, transparency efforts are complex social processes conditioned by negotiations and conflicts that often lead to paradoxical and surprising situations (Albu and Flyverbom, 2016). Therefore, transparency in organizational affairs is much more than the smooth transmission of information and we need other analytical starting points than whether the supplied information is good, plentiful and relevant enough. When companies like Enron, Siemens or Volkswagen turn out to be fraudulent and disappointing, our first reaction may be to focus on quality, quantity and relevance of the material they share with us. But the problems with these organizations were not a lack of information and scrutiny alone, and it is problematic if we reduce complex phenomena to information issues.

Organizations, objects and states of affairs do not exist in separation from the representations and communication activities we rely on, and this lack of a direct link requires that we develop other registers when talking about a phenomenon like transparency. Also, we need to remember that seeing, knowing and governing the conduct of organizations requires much more work. When organizations "go transparent" by installing digital and datafied systems that log everything and make it amenable to analysis, they also become responsible for that information. The ability to see inside their own operations and know almost everything about their employees, users and customers is both a blessing and a curse, and gives rise to hard questions about the management of visibilities. This chapter's conceptual and empirical explorations of these issues are an important starting point both if we want to grasp the potentials and limits of transparency efforts in organizational settings.

Levels of ambition when it comes to transparency differ markedly. In some organizations, disclosure is considered a necessary evil demanded by the authorities or others asking for information. However, the call for increased transparency comes not only from disappointed outsiders or regulators demanding better oversight. Some organizations push and peddle transparency ideals very actively and consider openness and legibility to be hallmarks of innovation and attraction. Focusing on the most determined ones shows just how complex and paradoxical transparency projects can be, and highlights some important dynamics involved in the organizational management of visibilities. This chapter takes internet companies as a starting point for a discussion of how organizations manage visibilities and position themselves vis-à-vis users, other organizations and the regulatory and political environments they operate in. Tech companies, such as Google, Facebook and others, are useful illustrations for my attempt to show how the management of visibilities shapes organizational affairs and relations between organizations and their surroundings. Also, the focus on internet companies allows me to bring out the complexities and dynamics of a wide range of visibility practices that cut to the core of what these companies are and do. Internet companies are both engaged in the *creation of publicity*, in the *keeping of secrets* and in the *pursuit of transparency*. When it comes to *publicity*, these companies and their founders take up a big place in the public domain, whether in the shape of news stories, popular movies or reports on the future of business. In many ways, we know these companies better than most. When it comes to *secrecy*, these companies are also very focused on keeping large parts of what they do to themselves. Google, for instance, refuses to disclose details about its earnings in individual countries. What internet companies use our digital traces for is also a trade secret, as are obviously new products and services before they launch. Furthermore, the secrecy of internet companies is highlighted in discussions about algorithms and other black-boxed aspects of their workings and business models (Pasquale, 2015). But these companies are also highly engaged in the pursuit of *transparency* as an organizational, political and societal ideal. That is, they stress the value of openness and sharing as organizational ideals, and they contribute to the present focus on access to information and disclosure as a source of accountability in public institutions and political affairs. At first glance, this may seem counterintuitive: how can companies be visible, secretive and transparent at the same time? But this is exactly the point that this book emphasizes, namely that we need to explore how different visibility practices and concerns come together, and how we – as individuals, organizations and societies – govern and are governed through such managed visibilities.

While the empirical and illustrative starting point is internet companies, we could say similar things about other types of organizations. Think, for instance, of terrorist organizations, such as Al-Queda and ISIS. They also thrive on their ability to create publicity, work in secret and in other ways manage visibilities in strategic and intricate ways (Stohl and Stohl, 2011). Similarly, many traditional types of organizations also engage in managing visibilities in numerous ways (Scott, 2013; Costas and Grey, 2016). Internet companies may be at the forefront of both the spread of transparency ideals and of the digital transformations that this book is about. Still, many points about the management of visibilities in organizational settings are also relevant for other business domains and types of organizations.

Internet companies are also central to the contemporary fascination with information as a source of clarity and human betterment, and contribute to the development and institutionalization of transparency as a societal and organizational ideal. This informational starting point takes a number of shapes. Fundamentally, digital platforms are sites for the compilation, structuring and mining of information, and the success of companies such as Google and Facebook starts from their ability to handle digital information in the most effective and appealing manner. As we know, the starting points of these companies were much more modest. Sergey Brin and Larry Page were PhD students at Stanford University, doing work on how to best retrieve and sort massive and rapidly changing amounts of digital information. In a conference paper from 1998, titled "The Anatomy of a Large-Scale Hypertextual Web Search Engine," they described their prototype, already then called Google, and suggested how it may solve many of the problems that existing, often manual, approaches to search faced. Facebook's early ambitions were also somewhat modest, namely a website called Facemash that compiled and paired photos from the university profiles of students and invited people to vote on "who was hotter." While the website was soon shut down by the university, the idea of a centralized site for all Harvard students was central to the site that Zuckerberg went on to develop, TheFacebook.com, and what later expanded into the world's biggest social media platform and beyond. While these histories of Google and Facebook may be well-known, they are worth bringing up because they point to the foundational ways in which the two companies have been able to cater to two important social needs, namely to find and organize information and to build and maintain relationships. It also reminds us that their roles as tech giants are in many ways a by-product of their success, and not a goal that they had from the outset. In fact, both companies spent years struggling financially and had no clear sense of how to make their inventions profitable. Advertising, which now makes up the core of both companies came into the equation rather late. In fact, Brin and Page warned against mixing search and advertising. As they stated, the "goals of the advertising business model do not always correspond to providing quality search to users" and warned against its potentially negative effects on the quality and accuracy of searches (Brin and Page, 1998: 18).

The centrality of organizing information and creating a better world through information is reflected in the mission statements of both companies. Google wants to "organize the world's information and make it universally accessible and useful," and Facebook seeks to "make the world more open and connected." While neither of these corporate missions makes explicit references to transparency, the connections between information, openness and a better world are all there – ambitions to organize information and make the world open are intrinsically tied to ideals about transparency. So even if phrased differently, the transparency formula, discussed in the Introduction, also underpins the missions and aspirations of digital platforms. They are intimately involved in the material development and ideational circulation of the doctrine that more and better information is the solution to the problems they implicitly refer to in their mission statements – the lack of access to information, the existence of information without structure, or the existence of a closed-off world without connections. In this respect, we can think of these companies as transparency machines and as part of a larger movement working to institutionalize the transparency formula – more information, more clarity and better governance. But it does not make sense to think of corporations like Google and Facebook as transparent organizations, or the world they seek to build or facilitate as a transparent one. What is at stake is a more fundamental and surprising set of developments that we need to pin down. My suggestion is that we need to think of the excitement about transparency as a force that makes the management of visibilities a key issue in a datafied world – an individual, organizational, and political matter of concern that we need to grapple with conceptually and empirically. To make sense of this, we can start by charting the relationships between organizational processes, transparency projects and managed visibilities. This involves going through different forms of visibility management in organizations to highlight their workings as forms of socialization, control and communication that make and shape organizations in a datafied world.

TRANSPARENCY AND ORGANIZATIONAL CULTURE

How do organizations engage people and create a sense of belonging and shared goals? For long, the response has been "organizational culture" – the sets of more or less explicit values and patterns of behavior that members of organizations share and reproduce (Schein, 1992; Ravasi and Schultz, 2006). The socialization of new employees largely happens by observing what others do and do not do, and by picking up established procedures and orientations. In some organizations, transparency ideals have become one component of such guidelines and worldviews. This is worth exploring both because it tells us something about the circulations and translations of transparency ideals as they travel across different social settings, and because it shows how transparency shapes organizational settings and create demands for the management of visibilities. US-based technology companies in particular have embraced transparency as an ideal and defining feature of their organizational cultures. Across policy statements, business development, relations with users and broader discussions about digital transformations, such companies propel narratives about the value of openness, information sharing and transparency. Other types of organizations in other sectors and parts of the world also embrace transparency ideals, but tech companies seem to more vocal and explicit in their adoption. In these settings, transparency ideals operate both as sources of socialization, and as ways to increase the attractiveness of the organizations vis-à-vis the world outside.

In the internet industry, ideals about transparency and openness play important roles in relation to organizational arrangements, policy developments, product design and advocacy. The aspiration to share information, allow for insight and scrutiny, and make organizational processes visible is increasingly part of the systems of belief that tech companies in particular hone and value. It obviously exists alongside and in tandem with other ideals and aspirations, such as innovation, "work as play," and other types of Silicon Valley logics (Turner, 2009). Also, transparency ideals drive a wide range of organizational choices and initiatives involving everything from office layouts, meeting formats and communication practices to relations between managers and employees. In the words of one Facebook director, transparency efforts in the company originate from Mark Zuckerberg's belief "that if we all understand the virtue of transparency we will do our jobs better."

If you walk around the Facebook main office, located on 1 Hacker Way in Menlo Park, California, you will notice that the large industrial-looking halls have only one kind of offices. Placed around large tables, so-called bullpens, employees work in open spaces with no cubicles or walls. This kind of office space is also what Mark Zuckerberg, Sheryl Sandberg and other directors and managers have in the company, and is described as a direct route to open communication. Still, there are meeting rooms available. Employees call the one preferred by Zuckerberg the "Aquarium," a label that obviously relies on and extends the discourse on glass, transparency and openness as a principle for organizational layout and culture. According to a Facebook director, this means that "Anyone, any visitor can come along in the corridor and see into the meeting that he may be having. So, he feels people should know what he is up to. There are no secrets and people can see what he is spending his time on and know what is the most important for the company." Also, another director at Facebook suggested to me that "hierarchy is in opposition to transparency." Here, as in many other organizational settings, possibilities for observation are cast as direct routes to transparency, because they enable "the public to gain information about the operations and structures of a given entity" (Etzioni, 2010: 1).

Transparency projects at Google and Facebook also focus on opportunities for employees and users to engage openly with top managers. At Google, there is a well-established tradition for so-called Thank God It's Friday (TGIF) meetings. These are organized as employee forums with short presentations about plans and developments, and room for open questions from employees. Like other management processes at Google, these weekly meetings are described as incarnations of the "default to open": They allow for "transparency and voice," and contribute to the creation of a work environment marked by sharing, engagement and insight. Similarly, Facebook's CEO Mark Zuckerberg regularly holds so-called Townhall Q&As where he responds to questions via Facebook for an hour. Such projects, which – explicitly and implicitly – work in the name of transparency, are highly popular among employees and users and are emphasized repeatedly by the companies involved. But they are also organizational situations of a particular kind: TGIFs are social events involving large numbers of employees on a Friday afternoon, and this format may invite particular kinds of questions and discourage others. What is said is not to be shared with outsiders: "We share everything, and trust Googlers to keep the information confidential," as a Google (2011) *Think People* newsletter puts it.

Also, we need to consider how responding to questions during an online Townhall Q&A is constrained by socio-material conditions such as navigating and selecting among 50,000–100,000 questions and comments within an hour. The point is that when organizations claim to be transparent, they are mainly managing visibilities. We cannot understand transparency projects without careful attention to the formats, processes of socialization and other affordances of the technologies and environments in which they play out, including the need for actors to act in certain ways (Flyverbom, 2016b).

Internal work processes are also described with reference to transparency in these companies. For instance, Facebook largely relies on the group functions that are available within their platform for communication among employees, rather than separate emails. In this manner, conversations are visible to more people, and insights can be used by others, which, according to the director, "creates this feeling of community, but also transparency internally." Similarly, very early on at Google, a lot of the information that more traditional organizations would consider personal was stored in a shared system called MOMA. Some companies take these ideas about the value of open communication to new levels, such as when the social media company Buffer experiments with sharing emails internally. As part of Buffer's "default to transparency," all emails are visible by default to all employees, although it is still possible to send direct, private messages. This is how the company describes the policy: "How would you like everyone on your team to see every email that you send? At Buffer, we love it! Our value of transparency extends all the way to the inbox. Every email is public within the team. Every bit of communication gets shared. Everyone knows everything. There are no secrets" (https://open.buffer.com/buffer-transparent-email/). The choice between transparency and secrecy, good and bad, may seem as straightforward as this. But as Birchall (2015; 2016) and Costas and Grey (2014; 2016) have shown in their work on the organizational workings of secrecy, there are good reasons to work with, rather seek to remove secrecy. Secrecy, they remind us, is a fundamental and important dimension of social and organizational life. If we never intentionally concealed information, such as product plans, political strategies or decisions about personal matters, many social arrange- ments would fall apart (Costas and Grey, 2016). But it is not only for practical purposes that we need spaces for secrecy. As Birchall (2015; 2016) suggests, the contemporary infatuation with transparency makes us forget that secrecy is also a valuable and productive social and political force. Furthermore, the juxtaposition of transparency and secrecy is problematic. Many parts of the literature on the topic define transparency as "simply the opposite of secrecy" (Coombs and Holladay, 2013: 217; Florini, 2001: 13) and distinguish sharply between transparency as "true" and secrecy as "intentional." But as this book, and other critical studies of transparency (Fenster, 2006;

Birchall, 2016) suggest, there are multiple similarities between transparency and other visibility practices, including secrecy. Not long after their transparency project was implemented, Buffer realized that people in the company had turned to sending mostly private messages: According to other material published by Buffer, only 30 percent of messages go through the public channel, and more than 60 percent are sent as direct messages, only to be seen by those interacting. This shows us that there is a need for privacy and opacity if people are to work efficiently. But it also shows the willingness to experiment with transparency efforts and to publish the results, even if surprising.

More generally, such efforts are regularly described as ways of building cultures of openness in organizations. When Google describes its organizational culture and management style, transparency is intimately connected to the cultivation of particular kinds of behavior and expectations from employees. Consider the following quotes from a Google newsletter article titled "Passion, Not Perks":

> If you're an organization that says "our people are our greatest
> asset," you must default to open. It's the only way to demonstrate to
> your employees that you believe they are trustworthy adults and
> have good judgment. And giving them more context about what is
> happening (and how, and why) will enable them to do their jobs
> more effectively and contribute in ways a top-down manager
> couldn't anticipate. . . . We regularly survey employees about their
> managers, and then use that information to publicly recognize the
> best managers and enlist them as teachers and role models for the
> next year. The worst managers receive intense coaching and
> support, which helps 75 percent of them get better within a quarter.
> *(Google, 2011)*

Many kinds of organizations actively work with and promote transparency projects. Such experiments with increased openness range from web sites where organizations share information about themselves, over blogs where CEOs or employees discuss their ideas or aspirations, to town hall meetings and other events made publicly accessible via live feeds. Despite the differences in shape and purpose, such initiatives all speak to the present infatuation with transparency as a hallmark of innovative and "good" organizations. More parts and processes of organizing are made legible and open to scrutiny from the outside, and sometimes with consequences. Internet companies such as Google and Facebook may stress their commitment to principles of transparency. But also users and critical voices in media and government call for increased transparency, just like the "transparency movement" (Sifry, 2011) epitomized by Wikileaks, Transparency International and the Sunlight Foundation, contributes to the institutionalization of transparency as an increasingly significant norm and form of conduct in the digital domain. These developments can help us grasp the importance and workings of transparency and managed visibilities in processes of organizing.

We can think of managed visibilities as similar to what is often described as organizational cultures. That is, more or less articulated forms of socialization and ways of working that help employees navigate and are used by organizations to position themselves vis-à-vis their surroundings. While the ambitions with transparency projects may be to optimize work, heighten legitimacy and build trust in organizations, such efforts also become part of the attempt to organize work, manage organizations and maintain relations with outsiders. Implicitly, such initiatives also serve to highlight the differences between companies that go transparent, and more traditional corporations marked by hierarchies and centralized communication. Transparency has become an important resource in such attempts at organizational identity formation and positioning. This means that managing visibilities becomes a fundamental, organizational activity. We will look at two ways in which the management of visibilities comes to shape organizational affairs. The first has to do with power and control, and involves attempts to position transparency as an end to control and a driver of more horizontal power relations. The second involves strategic uses of transparency and secrecy in the construction of organizational uniqueness and mysteriousness.

CONTROL BY VISIBILITY MANAGEMENT

"Secrets are lies," "privacy is theft" and "sharing is caring" are the slogans of the fictional tech company described by Dave Eggers (2014) in his book *The Circle*. When Mae, a young girl and the main character in the book, gets a job in this attractive company, she is more than thrilled. In fact, she thinks she is entering something resembling heaven. As the story unfolds, some more hellish sides of life in this company start to show. The company, which resembles large Silicon Valley companies like Google and Facebook, is obsessed with transparency. Employees' desks are packed with monitors and they are expected to report and share everything they do. Also, their performance is measured, ranked and made public. Even outside work, they are expected to let their colleagues know what they learn and experience, and the overall ambition of the company is to have enough high-quality information that they can "close the circle" – i.e. know everything about everyone and build a perfectly transparent organization and society (Flyverbom, Christensen and Hansen, 2015). Mae, like other employees, slowly gets invaded by this organization "gone transparent" where all parts of life are monitored, measured and made public. Even if few employees in actual organizations are pushed as hard as Mae and others in the Circle, the book highlights a more general point about the triumph of transparency and the quest for more scrutiny, openness and control made possible by digital technologies. Also, this dystopian fiction story about technologically driven and invasive forms of transparency is surprisingly similar to a number of real-life tech companies with similar transparency ambitions.

The tech company Buffer, for example, shares a wealth of information that is normally kept hidden within a company or only available to a small group of directors. With an explicit decision to share much "behind-the-scenes data and info" (Widrich, 2017), the company makes it possible for anyone to see the salaries of people employed, how stock options are distributed and how much money the company makes and spends, both in monthly and in real-time breakdowns.

Employees and their individual performance are one component of this push for transparency. Also, at Buffer everyone is equipped with a health tracker that measures and shares their sleep, nutrition and exercise patterns, and all employees are asked to share their plans for improved performance in a publicly accessible section of the company web site. Transparency, it seems, is a way to heighten engagement and productivity. As one of the directors puts it:

> One of our key values at Buffer is to work smarter, not harder. Personal improvement is a big part of that, so giving employees a tool that can help improve their sleep patterns is a no-brainer. A few weeks in it's already had an incredible effect. Browsing everyone's sleep patterns and talking about how to get more *deep sleep* has an amazing effect on productivity.
>
> *(Haden, 2013)*

Visibilities afforded by trackers then become part of organizational optimization projects.

Sharing performance improvement plans with colleagues is another initiative at Buffer pursued in the name of transparency. Using the publicly accessible site www.open.buffer.com, the "entire Buffer team starts each week fresh with new goals – both work and personal" (Seiter, 2014). For instance, one employee, Brian, promises to look after his diet, Neil wants to get more sleep and watch fewer series on Netflix and Joel has developed "six commandments" that he seeks to follow: daily exercise, early mornings and good sleep, thoughtful and deliberate eating, helping others via blogging and office hours, daily meditation, and reflection time via reading and walks. Others admit that they have not been consistent or successful in the improvement efforts, because they have been travelling or not focused enough. One employee, Colin, has therefore decided to go back to the ten core values of Buffer and use them to move forward: "Something

I've been meaning to do for a while is focus on the Buffer values. So, for this week and the next, I'm planning on one per day." On day one, Colin will "always choose positivity and happiness"; on day 2, "default to transparency"; on day 3, "have a focus on self improvement"; on day 4, "be a 'no ego' doer"; on day 5, "listen first, then listen more"; on day 6, "have a bias towards clarity"; on day 7, "make time to reflect"; on day 8, "live smarter, not harder"; on day 9, "show gratitude"; and finally on day 10, "do the right thing" (Seiter, 2014). These ten values describe the "The Buffer culture – powered by happiness," and seem to be circulated actively through the requirement that everyone has to respond to them in ways that are visible to everyone else at Buffer.

The example of Buffer allows us to consider what happens to work practices when organizations go transparent. Do people happily share and use all this information, does the organization become more knowable and knowledgeable and are organizational problems solved as a result? In the case of Buffer, there may be multiple benefits of these transparency efforts, at least from the perspective of optimization of employee performance. But they also put new demands on employees when it comes to managing visibilities, and they create unforeseen complications. Another experiment with transparency at Buffer focused on holidays. Taking time off at Buffer is seemingly easier than elsewhere: Employees can take as much holiday as they like, as long as they share their plans with everyone else, and preferably keep others updated on their holiday experience via social media. But, somewhat surprisingly, unlimited vacation time in combination with a default to transparency meant that only a small number of employees would go on holiday. Since the directors never took holidays, employees "could see it wasn't the norm" (Widrich, 2018) and would stay at their desk instead of taking advantage of the offer. In an attempt to change this situation, the company directors stressed that they "highly encourage each teammate to take at least a weeklong vacation every year," went on a holiday of their own, and even added a $1,000 bonus to encourage employees to do the same. Still, not all employees would take vacation and those who did would only go away for less than a week. As a result, Buffer has changed its holiday policy and now demands that all employees take a minimum of 15 days off every year.

These examples of organizational uses of transparency as a driver for optimization and control highlight both the excitement about transparency and the processes of visibility management that come into play. Showing, hiding and reacting to shared information becomes a central part of being and navigating in organizational settings.

The accentuation of visibility management processes as a result of digital transformations also has wide-reaching implications for many other organizational issues. For instance, law enforcement agencies around the Western world are busy implementing new systems for the aggregation, analysis and visualization of data about citizens. Such data-driven approaches are presently dominated by systems developed by Palantir Technologies, a Silicon Valley-based company started by Peter Thiel, who is also founder of PayPal and on the board of Facebook. The platform allows police departments and other law enforcement agencies to connect and integrate all their separate databases and explore patterns across these data. At the same time, however, the platform logs all activities of employees using the system. This means that organizations suddenly have fine-grained data on every possible breach of organizational rules or restrictions, and must consider how much they want to know. The dilemma is real: if you spend the time and other resources going through this material, mistakes and misconduct will surface and require action. And if you ignore or store the information and mistakes happen, critics and authorities will hold you accountable for your lack of action and attention. Data may become not only burdensome, but even toxic. At the core of these dilemmas are questions about the management of visibilities: with new technological possibilities for logging and accessing data, questions about what to see, what to show and what to leave in the dark move to the fore. Also, managing visibilities in organizational settings with an abundance of information requires not only organizational policies and decisions, but also individual ones. The systems offered by Palantir and similar companies have almost endless features and possibilities for scrutinizing and combining data – from internal databases about criminal records, standard information about citizens, social media scrapings and so much more – so decisions about what to look at and what to correlate becomes a matter of deliberate choice. The question is what happens to employees when technical restrictions are minimal and professional and ethical ones have to take center stage? As with other forms of visibility management, the responsibilities that employees have to take on are challenging and wide-reaching. As technology-driven transparency projects make their way into organizational settings, people need to take on new roles as data managers, data ethicists and other kinds of new professions that they may not be trained for. In the process, questions about how to manage visibilities become a foundational and pivotal concern for everyone in the organization.

MANAGED VISIBILITIES AS ORGANIZING FORCES

The imagined organization described in *The Circle* and the radical transparency initiatives at Buffer may be extreme. But fictional and experimental companies are not the only settings where organizations go to great lengths when it comes to transparency initiatives such as to open up, share information and otherwise pursue transparency. As transparency travels further, we may see similar developments in more traditional organizational settings.

The organizational experiments and concerns with transparency at big tech companies like Google and Facebook, smaller ones like Buffer and even fictional ones like the Circle are instructive for at least two reasons. They speak to the argument that transparency initiatives currently shape organizations in numerous and sometimes surprising ways. They also tell us something about the relationship between the management of visibilities and the workings of power and control. The point is not that transparency always contributes to control, but rather that we need to unpack the multiple workings of transparency and the forms of managed visibilities involved.

Coordination and control are fundamental concerns in organizational settings (Mumby, 2013). Goals and activities need to be aligned, and many organizations are focused on socializing employees into particular ways of working and thinking. Increasingly, transparency has become one way in which such coordination is carried out. This may seem counterintuitive because we have come to associate transparency with less control, with eliminating power asymmetries and with empowerment. That is, we often think of power as closely tied to secrecy or invisibility – power and control rely on being out of sight, not seeable. Just think of the discourse surrounding transparency: Making what is invisible visible by disclosing information is offered as a solution to problems such as the abuse of power. More transparency in the organizational realm leads to better behavior. But we need to problematize these simple associations between visibility and power. Transparency is not simply a solution to problems associated with power, but also a source of power and control. Thinking about transparency as a social process of managing visibilities, rather than a matter of disclosing information, makes questions about power and the shaping of conduct central. A basic definition of power is "the production, in and through social relations, of effects that shape the capacities of actors to determine their own circumstances and fate" (Barnett and Duvall, 2005: 4). Along these lines, we can think of transparency as a way to shape human conduct. The illustrations from organizations gone transparent are a useful starting point for understanding how the management of visibilities operates as a source of power and as a form of organizing or ordering. When employees at Buffer refrain from taking holidays, it is intimately tied to the kinds of visibilities made possible by transparency efforts. Since everyone sees that very few people take holidays and knows that taking one would be visible to others, an otherwise appealing offer remains untouched. We can think of this as an obvious form of control at a distance – the subtle ways in which humans' capacities and conditions for action are shaped by social forces. This reminds us that control is not direct and external, but indirect and internalized; for instance, when visibility management becomes a key concern in organizations. This is so because transparency projects are often open-ended and ambiguous, and therefore require extensive interpretive work. Transparency projects often revolve around strategic ambiguity; that is, "use ambiguity purposely to accomplish their goals" (Eisenberg, 1984: 230, see also Flyverbom, Christensen and Hansen, 2015). As a result, transparency efforts produce subtle forms of control that operate not only through observation but also through the shaping of conduct, identities and other aspects of human life in organizations (Thornborrow and Brown, 2009; Flyverbom, Christensen and Hansen, 2015). Or put differently, transparency and the forms of visibility management it gives rise to are important, 'performative forces in the shaping of organizational realities (Albu and Flyverbom, 2016; Flyverbom and Reinecke, 2017). This relationship between transparency, managed visibilities and control is an important dimension of organizational processes.

Also, many organizations increasingly consider transparency to be a central and important dimension of organizational excellence and attractiveness. In a range of organizational settings, such ambitions about transparency drive the crafting of extensive policies and procedures for the disclosure of information to employees, customers, and stakeholders, as well as other attempts to institutionalize transparency in and around organizations. It seems like technology companies are competing on how far they can go when it comes to transparency, and are also involved in various forms of what we can think of as "transparency evangelism." If these developments seep into other organizational settings and sectors, we will see a growing need for reflections on information control and the curation of data. The push for transparency not only has organizational ramifications, but also shapes societal and political developments more broadly, as we will see in Chapter 5.

Attraction by Visibility Management

The illustrations of the importance of transparency in organizational dynamics show how such ideas travel and guide organizational processes, and highlight some of the complications and ambiguities they come with. But, as suggested in Chapter 2, we should not investigate transparency without looking at its attendant issues – secrecy, opacity and other visibility practices. One starting point is to consider the importance of secrecy as an organizational phenomenon. In many ways, secrecy works in tandem with transparency when it comes to positioning these organizations as unique and enticing. Put differently, a *lack* of transparency supports attempts to brand a company as an attractive and cutting-edge edge place to work, and to create curiosity and excitement about products and innovations. As Schein's (1992) classic work on organizational culture reminds us, mysteriousness and boundaries are central to organizational life (see also Flyverbom, Christensen and Hansen, 2015, and Costas and Grey, 2016). That is, secrecy and mysteriousness seem to work as an effective strategy if you want outsiders to be excited about your products or organizations, and the management of what people can see and peek into is a key dimension of creating such forms of attraction. In the internet industry and beyond, such negotiations over transparency, secrecy and other visibilities are at play in product launches, information sharing about strategies and innovation, and a driving force in the creation of a market for books such as *What Would Google Do?* (Jarvis, 2009) or *In the Plex: How Google Thinks, Works, and Shapes Our Lives* (Levy, 2011) that promise us a peek inside the heads and labs of such companies.

Entering most technology companies requires an invitation and that you sign a non-disclosure agreement (NDA) promising not to tell the outside world about what you hear or see inside. For instance, at Google's headquarters in Mountain View – the

Googleplex – or Facebook's buildings in Menlo Park, one does not get beyond the reception desk without such agreements in place. Having entered your name, host and the purpose of your visit at reception, you are asked to sign an NDA stating that no confidential information obtained on the premises may be disclosed, including "the existence of this Agreement and the fact or nature of the discussions between the parties" (Facebook Single Party Non-Disclosure Agreement), or that the agreement "supersedes all prior oral and written agreements" (Google Non-Disclosure Agreement). This is a formal type of visibility management, explicating a clear boundary between the inside and outside of these companies, and between what can be shared and what needs to remain confidential.

These observations about the spread of and limits to transparency in internet companies epitomize some of the tensions involved when visibility management becomes a key organizational issue. In organizations and elsewhere, a commitment to transparency is not the same as full disclosure or openness, so the negotiation of what to make visible and highlight, and what to keep opaque and out of sight, becomes an intriguing issue to focus on. These observations pave the way for the focus on the entanglements and complications involved in the crystallization of transparency as a norm and form of ordering in the internet industry.

There is nothing surprising or controversial about this. All sorts of organizations have things to hide or keep to themselves, and running any sort of social collective requires spaces for intimacy and privacy. In the context of tech companies, the obsession with NDAs and other ways of managing visibilities has multiple facets: Product development and innovation requires peace and space for testing and maintaining intellectual property rights and possibilities for uninterrupted and hidden work. At the same time, the management of visibilities adds to the mystique and sense of innovativeness that tech companies thrive on in the imagination of the public, their customers and competitors.

There are multiple dynamics at work when internet companies such as Google and Facebook actively seek to position themselves as transparent organizations – built on and managed by principles such as information sharing, employee participation and openness. Transparency has become one component of the attempts to position these organizations as different from traditional corporations. Managed visibilities are intimately involved in the creation of organizational cultures and norms and in attempts to position companies in particular ways. In such contexts, the management of visibilities often involves careful balancing of the attraction of openness and involvement and the attraction produced by a degree of opacity and secrecy to spur myth-building. These forms of visibility management contribute to the strategic positioning of organizations as different, or even as celebrity organizations seeking to attract attention and interest (Rindova, Pollock and Hayward, 2006).

COMMUNICATION AND THE TRANSPARENT ORGANIZATION

Contacting an internet company like Google or Facebook is not easy. There is no "about" section on their sites, and their nature as digital platforms means that their web sites *are* their main presence, and not merely a place to find their employees or get in touch with them. As a result, possibilities for contacting the companies are often placed in more specialized areas of the sites, and mostly possible for those who have a commercial relation with the company. If you have a problem with Google AdWords, help may be available. But as a normal user, a researcher or journalist, you will rarely get a response and as much communication as possible is set up to be automated or solved through user forums, where other users may offer you help. Such decisions make sense when you think about the volume of queries and interactions with millions of users, but they are also an indication that tech companies spend their resources on other things. Employees are costly and if automated systems or other users can handle these tasks, tech companies can focus on research and development, as well as keeping competitors at bay. While more hands-on approaches to content moderation and user engagement are on the rise, particularly after the Cambridge Analytica scandal, tech companies seem to always opt for automated systems and technical solutions, rather than human labor. Also, in other ways, digital platforms do not behave like "normal" companies when it comes to managing communication. When these companies become involved in big news stories or come under attack from disappointed users or critical public figures, their first response is often to have a more or less marginal employee or a consultant from an external public affairs agency comment publicly. But they are also indicative of a set of more fundamental issues about communication and control in digital spaces.

Traditional ways of handling communication activities in organizational settings often rely on a particular group of people or a dedicated department in charge. Such centralized approaches to communication are often driven by a wish to ensure quality, consistency and other forms of control. If all communication activities are handled in one place, messages can be aligned, and organizations can speak with one voice. But active and engaging forms of communication with users, customers and stakeholders are rarely as orderly as these centralized approaches tend to assume. Some organizations may still rely on the periodical newsletter or a targeted press release where they decide on the message, the audience and the time of publication. Most communication, however, takes place elsewhere and is much harder to control. As a result of developments in digital technology, communication activities are increasingly difficult to contain in particular departments or parts of organizations. Producing and circulating content is easy, and digital technologies allow many members of an organization to edit and develop communication products (Treem and Leonardi, 2013). In the case of Google, such decentralized approaches when it comes to communication are supported through the decision to ask different projects and initiatives within the organization set up individual blogs and web sites to engage directly with users and interested parties. In the words of the policy director, Google has a belief in the value of "very little centralized control over information flows." This decentralized approach to communication, including more than 50 different project blogs, means that "lots of people are speaking on behalf of the company" (interview with policy director, 2011). As a Google newsletter states, the company seeks to "share everything, and trust Googlers to keep the information confidential" (Google, 2011: 1). This approach means that crucial decisions about visibility management are delegated to employees and team leaders, and requires that they are able to identify and manage the boundary between the inside and outside of the organization. Sometimes, however, mistakes happen, and such situations are helpful if we want to understand the workings of communication in organizations claiming to be transparent. In the case of Google and Facebook, their commitment to transparency is tested when information leaks to unintended audiences. This may happen before product launches, but also when internal messages are made public by mistake or by critical employees. One example is when Google attempted to become a stronger social networking player by launching the service Google+, hoping to take a share of Facebook's dominance in the area and gain access to more social data. One of the engineers involved in the development of Google+ shared his frustrations with the initiative. As he put it, "Google+ is a prime example of our complete failure to understand platforms from the very highest levels of executive leadership (hi Larry, Sergey, Eric, Vic, howdy howdy) down to the very lowest leaf workers (hey yo). We all don't get it." (Yegge, 2011). However, instead of posting the message internally as planned, he made it public through Google+ by mistake. Clearly, this violated the expectation that Google employees keep certain information confidential, and it made internal critique visible to the outside at a crucial stage of product development. But once organizations have committed to transparency and decentralized communication approaches, situations like these also require new approaches. Rather than punish or fire the engineer, the company allowed him to acknowledge the mistake and, in the process, show its commitment to transparency. The engineer described the company's reaction in this manner:

> Amazingly, nothing bad happened to me at Google. Everyone just laughed a lot, all the way to the top, for having committed what must be the greatgranddaddy of all Reply-All screw-ups in tech history. But they also listened, which is super cool. I probably shouldn't talk much about it, but they are already figuring out how to deal with some of the issues I raised. I guess I shouldn't be surprised, though. When I claimed in my internal post that "Google does everything right," I meant it. When they are faced with any problem at all, whether it's technical or organizational or cultural, they set out to solve it in a first-class way.
>
> *(Yegge, 2011)*

We may interpret this situation as an indication that Google is committed to transparency and provides room for the sorts of mistakes that a decentralized approach to communication may lead to. But it also speaks to the point that in organizations striving for transparency, the management of visibilities becomes a key issue and often an individual responsibility for a wide range of employees whose primary responsibilities and competencies lie elsewhere. Navigating the boundary between the inside and the outside of the organization is no longer a matter of following formal organizational policies and procedures, but a matter of developing individual judgments and skills. In the words of Google's policy director, this is in line with the company's ambition to be "processually transparent" rather than "substantially transparent," that is, to encourage transparency broadly without defining in advance what to disclose or how to present things. As a result of this strategy, judgments and responsibilities when it comes are managing visibilities are redistributed from top managers to team leaders and individual employees.

The acceptance of leaks and mistakes is not always the norm in organizations claiming transparency, and from time to time, stories about more heavy-handed approaches seep out of companies such as

Google and Facebook. For instance, in 2016, a former employee of Google filed a lawsuit because of what was termed an "internal spying program" at work in the company. The lawsuit, which was refuted as "baseless" by Google, argued that the program relied on employees voluntarily reporting on other employees who might have leaked information (Albergotti, 2011). Also at Facebook, stories about the limits to transparency commitments sometimes show up in the press. For instance, in the wake of concerns about Facebook's role in the election of President Trump, fake news and suggestions that the company favored some kinds of political contents over others, the magazine *WIRED* published a story outlining how a contract worker, hired to moderate Facebook's Trending Topics, forwarded screenshots of internal memos to a journalist. He was swiftly fired, and so were others he had interacted with over a message service called GChat, apparently accessible to Facebook's investigation teams (Thompson and Vogelstein, 2018). While all companies need to protect internal communications, organizations with advanced digital infrastructures have multiple ways of keeping track of what employees do and are able to act swiftly on this information.

Organizational transparency implies an individualization of responsibility when it comes to managing visibilities. Knowing what to disclose or hold back, what genre or narrative to rely on, and who you are writing for or will be read by then become central concerns for a larger number of organizational members. Down the road, such skills may become more prevalent, but in many cases employees are hired because of other competencies, and may be neither ready for the task of managing visibilities, nor aware of the extent of the responsibilities involved. Curating and controlling information becomes a primary skill, and as the following section highlights, such work is a central but somewhat overlooked dimension of digital transformations in organizations.

VISIBILITY MANAGEMENT BEHIND THE SCENES

Social media sites and other digital spaces are comfortable places to spend time. They offer us entertaining, fun or thought-provoking material, or simply the information we need. But we tend to forget that what we see and what we do not see are the results of careful curation and very strategic decisions. Social media platforms are edited, and to some degree editors of human realities. That is, they make some parts of human life, culture and history visible, and keep some parts out of sight, and this is why their content moderation practices can be understood as a form of visibility management. To approach digital spaces along these lines of thinking challenges the widespread perception that internet companies offer us automated, neutral systems that allow us to find and distribute information. What they do, rather, is to shape social and political affairs in somewhat hidden ways. These editing processes and their organizational consequences are the focus of this section.

Despite their rapid growth and ubiquitous presence, we rarely consider what kind of social spaces tech companies invite us to be part of. Platforms such as Facebook, YouTube and others are easy to use, actively invite you to sign up, and help you coordinate a wide range of tasks. With appealing interfaces and smart features that make existing organizational IT systems seem like ancient and evil obstructions, social media platforms are comfortable places. In many ways, they thrive on and extend our early expectations about the internet as a space for dialogue, engagement and human progress. Here, finally, is a place where everyone can voice their opinions, find the information they need and get in touch with strangers or old friends. In combination with the warm feelings expressed via likes, high-quality pictures of beautiful sunsets and entertainment in the shape of funny videos, they are great places to be. Obviously, some people enter these spaces with less benign goals in mind, some are angered by what they see and others use them for hateful attacks. However, these are not the primary uses that social media spaces are designed for, and their owners go to great lengths to create particular atmospheres, maintain standards for use and react to what they consider improper activities. Homophobic, violent and racist content is not supposed to be part of our experience in these spaces, and internet companies seek to keep it out of sight. A lot of contents and activities never even make it to our Google search, our Facebook feed or the stream of videos on YouTube. The work that this maintenance requires is largely invisible. No one tells us why particular content disappears, and once people are blocked from a platform, they cannot explain themselves any longer. The processes of content moderation that make this possible are worth exploring, especially because they are a key component of organizational attempts to manage visibilities.

As Gillespie (2017b: 5) reminds us, social media are not neutral platforms simply offering us a space for self-expression:

> These structures are certainly not neutral: they are designed to invite and shape participation, toward particular ends. This includes what kind of participation they invite and encourage; what gets displayed first or most prominently; how the platforms design navigation from content to user to exchange; the pressures exerted by pricing and revenue models; and how they organize information through algorithmic sorting, privileging some content over others, in opaque ways. And it includes what is not permitted, and how and why they police objectionable content and behavior.

Content moderation largely takes the shape of automated systems and procedures that allow users to flag content that they may find problematic. With billions of users and constant additions of massive streams of information, manual processing would be very costly and labor intensive. Most internet companies are thinly staffed compared to traditional workplaces. In fact, while tech companies such as Apple, Google, Microsoft, Cisco and Facebook make up a major part of the US economy, they employ very few people compared to more traditional companies like Walmart and car manufacturing companies. The people they employ are primarily engineers, designers and developers engaged in building new products and features. When it comes to maintaining and running their platforms, much of the work is automated and carried out by as few people as possible. Much of this is obviously caused by the nature of their business models, in particular when it comes to social media platforms. As they do not produce content, but facilitate the sharing of material and organize access to information, the nature of the work is obviously different from that of a traditional manufacturing company and other technology companies.

Data Janitors and Human Moderators

Many of the otherwise labor-intense processes involved in the aggregation, sorting and visualization of information are automated in internet companies. Algorithms, machine learning and similar kinds of automation are fundamental to such companies, and play a number of roles. Obviously, they make it possible to handle information masses at the scale and speed characterizing digital spaces. In line with this focus on technological solutions, internet companies have been successful at making us think of algorithms as technical, consistent and neutral sorting mechanisms. They are machines that sift through data, find patterns and present those to us in an impartial manner. Services like the now defunct Facebook Trending Topics offered us what we or similar users were interested in and talking about, in combination with news stories taken from other sources, and provided a personalized overview of the news stories of the day – an enhanced version of what we would normally get from our newspapers or TV. But the more Facebook starts to look like a news provider, the more "we start asking the same questions about editorial processes, biases and accountability that we have asked newspapers and other news outlets in the past" (Gillespie, 2016). What surprised many when stories about Facebook's editing of Trending Topics surfaced in the news was that many of the decisions about what to highlight as a trend or how to categorize particular issues were not made by algorithms, but rather human beings. These parts of the operations of internet companies often remain hidden to the public gaze. What these news stories showed was that Facebook relied on teams of contract workers curating contents and training algorithms to be able to select the right news stories. Such work is done in a number of different ways.

Thanks to news stories and the work of scholars like Roberts (2016), we are starting to understand the emotionally straining work done by "data janitors" who clean up social media platforms so users do not encounter extreme violence and other offensive material when scrolling through their Facebook feed or watching a video on YouTube. This work of managing visibilities is important to understand both because it shapes the digital spaces we engage with and because it constitutes a kind of hidden labor with wide-reaching ramifications for the people involved. We know very little about their work, their value or status in these companies and the extent to which these forms of human sorting and decision-making shape what is made visible, hidden and or simply disregarded on digital platforms. In some social media platforms, there will be in-house teams in charge of maintenance and cleaning, while others rely on contract workers or micro-labor websites such as Amazon's Mechanical Turk (Roberts, 2016). Part of what we have learned is that there are guidelines and manuals available for the workers involved in the editing, categorization and presentation of online contents. Such forms of hand-held and automated content moderation come to shape news feeds, the content we see on Facebook or the presentation of search results. And they are important because they help us understand how digital spaces are put together and presented, that is, how they manage visibilities for strategic purposes. These issues also speak to the bigger issue of neutrality. Not so long ago, it seemed like we could take for granted that, for instance, Google would treat all data equally, and offer us relevant results based on our profiles, without pushing selected results to the top or otherwise let special interests shape the flow of information. But there is a growing concern – voiced by commentators, US President Trump and European regulators – that Google seems to make some results, its own products and some political views more visible than others. These concerns revolve around what digital platforms do with the material that they do not want us to see, who makes these decisions and on what basis and with which potential biases? The question here is about the trustworthiness of digital platforms and about how political orientations and normative stands play a role in the management of visibilities and in the guidance of our attention. Such discussions have mainly been about whether content is treated equally or if some content is favored over others based on commercial or political interests, and how political orientations are shaped as a result. But the questions run much deeper, and involve issues such as how digital spaces develop the criteria by which data is sorted, how data are structured and what kinds of information ecosystems and forms of social ordering they lead to (Flyverbom and Murray, 2018).

The reliance on automated processes and the relatively low number of employees also puts these companies in a particular position when it comes to assessing their value and in the context of sales. If internet companies are seen as technological platforms and automated solutions, and not labor-heavy organizations, they may be valued higher by investors and others focusing on scalability and possibilities for rapid transfers and implementation in other settings. Put differently, it is an advantage for stock prizes and company sales if your company comes across as an advanced, technology-based utility, rather than a complex organization with lots of people and other organizational complications in need of attention. That is why the focus on automated processes and technologies, not people, make a lot of sense when internet companies go on the stock market or are sold. They downplay the role of human labor either by hiding it in invisible parts of the production chain, or by relying on temporary contract workers who do not show up as part of the company.

Content Moderation in Digital Spaces

Content moderation takes the shape of automated systems and human labor, and both kinds of work are hidden. The focus on moderation, editing and curation is important, and the different approaches involved are not as different as they may seem. Algorithms are not neutral, consistent or necessarily advanced forms of artificial intelligence. They are sorting procedures developed by humans, their choices and decisions are taught to them by humans and they rarely deliver results or make decisions on their own. Rather, they are shaped by human decisions and the results they deliver are the outcome of extensive interactions between humans and machines. As Gillespie (2016) puts it: "We prefer the idea that algorithms run on their own, free of the messy bias, subjectivity, and political aims of people. It's a seductive and persistent myth, one Facebook has enjoyed and propagated. But it's simply false." At the same time, the human labor that goes into content moderation is guided by relatively clear guidelines and procedures for the sorting of data and decisions about what to allow and what to remove. Taken together, these forms of editing and curating constitute an important and somewhat overlooked part of digital spaces. In particular, they are worth exploring because they give us valuable insights into the forms of visibility management that internet companies engage in, and how the results come to order social affairs. All these issues – largely about the management of visibilities – invite us to question, even "directly contradict myths of the Internet as a site for free, unmediated expression" (Roberts, 2016: 2). Social media platforms rely on more human labor than they tell us, and quite a number of features require human interventions from time to time.

To most people, the internet comes across as an open, ungoverned space where users can engage directly, and where everything is available in raw form. But social media sites are edited spaces, and in ways that go far beyond design features and interfaces. Content moderation balances profit-seeking and brand protection very carefully. Since most social media platforms rely on advertising as their primary source of revenue, a high number of users and interactions with content are central. Since the material that engages users most is often shocking or sensationalist in nature, some violence, bad language and other borderline content is worth having on the sites (Roberts, 2016). Still, too much shocking content in digital spaces will damage the reputation of the company and drive users away, and these are the concerns that content moderators have to balance.

These forms of curation and their intersections with the politics and economies of social media sites contribute to the argument about the importance of managing visibilities. Content moderation creates a particular kind of experience and guides our attention in digital spaces. Just like we rarely encounter the men and women cleaning our subway stations and streets, data janitors operate in the dark, in the basements of flashy and colorful headquarters of the internet giants, or via short-term contracts. This hidden industry of internet janitors and cleaning ladies makes sure that the platforms and sights we encounter are pleasant and in line with the values that shape those environments, such as a focus on expression of opinions, sharing of fun, social content and dialogue of a positive kind.

These issues are central to discussions of managed visibilities and highlight the work that goes into staging digital spaces as engaging, inviting and comfortable. More broadly, these issues are important because, with the majority of social data in the hands of privately owned and operated spaces, digital platforms shape key activities and domains in society. Friendships and social connections rely on Facebook, we can hardly access information without the help of Google search engines, and Amazon dominates online commerce. It is in the interest of these companies to come across as neutral, technological utilities, rather than biased or political actors. Such an image is good for valuations and good for staying out of public scrutiny and regulation. In the wake of news stories about the role of Facebook in BREXIT, the election of President Trump and the kinds of manipulation carried out by Cambridge Analytica, such images are hard to sustain. While such scandals may fade in the memories of the public and policymakers, the more fundamental questions about how data are structured and digital spaces are moderated will remain salient. And a focus on the management of visibilities offers a vocabulary for such investigations.

The more we think that information is processed by impartial machines, the more we are willing and able to see these digital platforms as neutral and necessary infrastructures. Social media sites are not neutral, open spaces, because they order the social by organizing information, guiding our attention and editing social realities. If we accept these biases and hidden operations now, they will likely become more engrained and invisible in the future.

TRANSPARENCY AS ORGANIZING FORCE

Contributing to the overall argument of this book, these illustrations from organizational settings allow us to problematize the simple equation between more information, clearer insight and better conduct and control that underpins much research on transparency. As soon as you look a little closer at actual transparency projects in organizational settings, they are a lot more complicated. Rather than clear-cut problem-solving or improvement, transparency efforts also have unintended consequences and paradoxical effects. This is why we need to think differently about transparency, as processes of managing visibilities and as processes of performative communication, and not simply as a matter of transmitting information and verifying or improving a particular state of affairs. If we push beyond the narrow focus on the transmission of information, transparency can be seen as a social and more extensive set of processes involving a wide range of actors, mediations and mutations. Transparency involves not only ongoing considerations about what to show and what to keep out sight, but also a number of uncertainties and complications. If we widen the scope and consider transparency efforts to be complex communication phenomena, we also become aware of how subjects, objects, technologies and settings play parts in the production of transparency. Understood in this manner, it also becomes more plausible that transparency processes are intricate configurations of visibilities that play a central role in the making and transformation of organizations. Along these lines, transparency efforts have performative effects that we need to come to terms with and integrate into existing work in the field. For instance, in work on organizational communication, digital technologies have been seen as engines of transparency and knowledge-sharing in organizations. They would make work processes, co-workers and information streams more identifiable, present and visible. Digital technologies and transparency efforts, however, do not simply produce clarity and visibilities, but also lead to complications and have effects other than recognition and empowerment (Brighenti, 2010). Also, we should include a much wider range of types of visibility practices when we consider the organizational workings of transparency – it cannot be separated from the broader set of visibility practices it operates in conjunction with: discussions of surveillance, transparency, leaks, opacity and secrecy can start from a more general focus on managed visibilities.

The management of visibilities and the guidance of attention are also new vocabularies for talking about the power of internet companies. This focus pushes us beyond widespread discussions about their monopolizing approaches and commercial dominance, concerns about their hunger for data and their ambitions to take over other industries and how they snoop on us and threaten privacy. The value of considering how they manage visibilities is more than that we get to understand them better as organizations. It also helps us articulate how they carry out unprecedented forms of curation and information control, manage visibilities on behalf of people and guide our attention in just about all spheres of social life. These questions about the sociopolitical consequences of managed visibilities are what we turn to now.

5   Seeing the World

As suggested throughout this book, digital transformations do not simply make individuals, organizations or societies more transparent. What happens is rather an intensification of the need to manage visibilities – to consider what to make (in)visible and how to guide attention. So far, my main concern has been to suggest what these developments mean for individuals and organizations, but now the focus shifts to broader societal issues. That is, how do hopes about digital transparency and processes of visibility management shape the way we think about societies and political affairs? Looking at such different phenomena as state control, corporate reporting, social editing and attempts to govern future affairs, the chapter offers an account of visibility management as a form of social ordering.

There is an important historical backdrop to this. Transparency is intimately tied to the project of modernity – the hope for technological progress, human perfectability and scientific scrutiny and rationality. But transparency is also an Enlightenment ideal that largely remains unchallenged, despite its limitations and obvious ties to phenomena such as totalitarianism and surveillance. What we see is the circulation of "messianic ideals" of transparency (Beyes and Pias, 2014) or what we may think of as a form of transparency evangelism. As Mehrpouya and Djelic (2014: 1) suggest, modern history is underpinned by "multiple competing and conflicting mobilizations of the notion of transparency through time to liberate, to deliberate, to legitimize, to control, to structure or to govern." Assessing these limits of transparency and articulating the dynamics of visibility management seem timelier than ever, and is not merely a conceptual or abstract endeavor. Our ideas about and dealings with transparency go beyond individual and organizational activities and have societal and political consequences. Explorations of transparency and the management of visibilities in societal and political affairs offer a way to consider what kind of societies and politics we may be developing. Picking apart the transparency formula as a form of social ordering is the final step in this books' attempt to grapple with the promises about societal progress and futures made in the name of transparency. Ultimately, the ambition is to articulate that the management of visibilities is inseparable from our understanding and ordering of the social and political worlds we inhabit.

STATE CONTROL: WATCHING CITIZENS AND GOVERNMENTS

States need to know their citizens, and throughout history, governments have developed extensive systems, such as censuses and ID cards, allowing them to count and keep track of people. But states also engage in other kinds of visibility practices, and citizens expect to be able to see what the state does. Transparency ideals are central to the democratic project of making governments accountable and involving citizens not only in the election of public officials, but also in the oversight of the operations of governments. As Hong and Allard-Huver (2016) put it, "transparency promises a 'virtuous chain' of informed citizens, rational deliberation and democratic participation." Such aspirations have been institutionalized in numerous ways. Modern democracies have adopted a range of practices when it comes to information sharing and public scrutiny of state documents. Freedom of Information Acts have evolved since the 1940s, and spread to many parts of the world (Fenster, 2012; Schudson, 2015). Such acts facilitate extensive forms of access to government files and decision-making processes and allow citizens to request multiple kinds of information. While such ideas have a long history and have been incorporated into the runnings of states, they also surface as political innovations or democratic promises. For instance, one of the key messages offered by Barack Obama (2009) in his US presidency was that he would create an "unprecedented level of openness in government." This initiative took its first shape as a memorandum titled "Transparency and Open Government" and the creation of the data-gov database where public information, tools and other digital resources were made available. Containing close to 200,000 datasets, this initiative has become emblematic of the contemporary obsession with transparency and information disclosure, and many other states have institutionalized similar programs. But at the same time, we cannot understand these transparency projects in separation from the other ways in which states control information and manage visibilities. President Obama did not set out to replace secrecy, surveillance and other established state practices with full transparency, and Birchall (2015: 186) and others have pointed to "the hypocrisy of Obama's simultaneous investment in secret statecraft and government transparency." Her point is not simply that we should condemn the gap between rhetoric and reality in situations like this, but rather that these kinds of transparency projects invite us to consider the intersections of transparency and secrecy and the kinds of demands and expectations they come with. Such developments lay new demands on citizens – we are expected to not only vote for or against particular individuals, but to engage much more in the workings and intricacies of the state by sharing and managing information and visibilities. As Birchall (2015) has reminded us, transparency projects implicitly rely on citizens to be active, entrepreneurial, and accountant-like when it comes to engaging with all these open data. In the process, they also become involved in and more responsible for the legitimacy and proper working of the state.

A number of international organizations have been central to the freedom of information agenda and the "transparency movement" (Sifry, 2011). Transparency International is probably the biggest of these organizations, but the Sunlight Foundation – which pursues "better governance through technology-empowered citizenship" (Klein, 2016) – and others have also contributed to the institutionalization of freedom of information initiatives. In more recent times, the emergence of internet-based sites such as WikiLeaks has given new impetus to such calls for transparency of state matters. While Freedom of Information Acts are initiated by states, more radical forms of disclosure have been driven by whistleblowers and others from the margins of organizations. In both institutionalized and fluid spaces, the management of visibilities is a key concern.

TRANSPARENCY IN POLITICAL AFFAIRS

The history of politics involves many spectacular cases where secret or otherwise hidden information was leaked to the public. The Watergate scandal and the leaking of the Pentagon papers in the early 1970s figure prominently in US politics, and shaped public perceptions of government affairs profoundly. In more recent times, the most spectacular of such outpourings of secret material began with WikiLeaks. Inviting journalists and whistleblowers to share classified material through a protected digital platform, WikiLeaks signaled the beginning of an era where the inner workings and logics of states got exposed publicly. For instance, the files and videos leaked by Manning in 2010 propelled WikiLeaks into the public domain and highlighted how digital technologies allow for new forms of disclosure and leaking. WikiLeaks lost momentum with the criminal allegations against its founder, Julian Assange, in 2012 and his continued political asylum in the Equadorian embassy in London. But other organizations and whistleblowers have followed suit. The Snowden revelations of the NSA surveillance programs and the so-called Panama Papers exposing global tax evasion schemes also show that radical forms of disclosure are still pursued despite the risks. Also, a growing number of digital platforms offer secure and anonymous possibilities for leaking and sharing, such as Globaleaks and SecureDrop. These developments often evoke hopes about digital technologies as solutions to long-standing problems, such as in Greenberg's (2012) book with the enthusiastic title *These Machines Kill Secrets*. As Heemsbergen (2016: 140) suggests, digitally mediated forms of leaking are often seen as clear-cut ends to secrecy: "Radical transparency in these configurations unapologetically uncovers what is true, holding to account those who would deceive. Openness wins." Along similar lines, various crime prevention efforts, such as anti-corruption and anti-money laundering efforts, have pushed for transparency principles to be institutionalized worldwide. Obviously, such initiatives are important and necessary. But this should not inhibit questions and reflections of a more critical nature, particularly because they may lead to better outcomes. As a program for the improvement of politics and societies, transparency takes largely proselytizing forms – i.e. a "radical social premise – that an inevitable enveloping transparency will overtake modern life" (Kirkpatrick, 2010: 200). But the consequences of these pushes for transparency at the level of states and international organizations are not simply more and better information. Just like individuals and organizations, social and political systems also have a hard time operating without some degree of secrecy. In the context of political negotiations and deal making, we see the emergence of procedures that allow for degrees of secrecy. These include ways to facilitate open dialogue in negotiations, such as Chatham House Rules, i.e. the agreement that participants may disclose *what* is said, but not *who* said it, after a meeting. Another example is the emergence of pre-meetings or non-meetings in contexts where all meetings have to be publicly accessible or viewable via recordings (Christensen and Cheney, 2015). Some experiment with doing politics in ways that adhere to strict principles about transparency. For instance, the German Pirate Party, founded in 2006, posited transparency as central to its aspirations. In all its operations, the Pirate Party considered "transparency as a right and a duty: a right for every member to express their opinions publicly without any restriction and a moral duty for party officials to document decision-making processes as well as all discussions in councils or committees" (Ringel, 2018: 15). But the decision that "everything has to be transparent" (ibid.) soon created a wealth of complications: disagreements and disputes among party members became visible to supporters and critics alike, masses of unfiltered information reached journalists and the public, and other parties became unwilling to collaborate with the Pirate Party because they could have no backstage conversations (ibid.). As a result of these unintended consequences of the commitment to transparency, the Pirate Party developed more nuanced approaches, for instance by distinguishing "between *political, strategic, practical* and *personal matters*" (ibid.: 31) and allowing these to be disclosed differently. As suggested throughout this book, what may start as a dream about transparency always ends up as a practical matter of managing visibilities. In the case of the German Pirate Party, navigating these terrains required a much more elaborate set of principles and practices related to information control, such as developing what Ringel (2018) refers to as both frontstage and backstage situations, and intricate relations between transparency and secrecy.

In other contexts, transparency efforts also involve important dynamics that may be overlooked if we trust the formula that more information gives more insight and better conduct. The work of Fenster (2015) speaks to this point. As he suggests, the trust in transparency as an administrative norm – a way to run institutions and societies – takes for granted that:

> 1. Government constitutes a producer and repository of information, one that can be made to send that information. 2. Government information constitutes a message that can be isolated and disclosed. 3. There is a public that awaits disclosure of government information and is ready, willing, and able to act in predictable, informed ways in response to the disclosure of state information."
>
> *(Fenster, 2015: 152)*

These assumptions consider transparency to be a simple matter of transmitting information. But as Fenster also suggests, transparency projects are more complex communication phenomena and this requires more nuanced understandings. Firstly, it is problematic to consider the state to be one thing. States, like other organizations and institutions contain people with very different roles and affiliations, conflicting logics and differentiated possibilities for information control (Fenster, 2015). This complexity and permeability makes it impossible to be a clear-cut source or solid container of information. Similarly, a communication approach reminds us that information cannot simply be packaged, transmitted and understood in a singular, unified manner. It is always subject to mediations and interpretations that may differ from one context to another. As Fenster (2015: 157) puts it, any "government document is polysemic, capable not only of different, partisan interpretations but also of willful reinterpretation by radical critics of the state." Finally, transparency projects expect all citizens to interpret information in a similar way. That is: "Transparency's theory of communication posits a public that awaits illumination: a nascent polis prepared to receive, interpret, and act upon the information revealed by the state's disclosures" (Fenster, 2015: 161). But publics may react to state disclosures in less rational, deliberative ways, or may not even be interested.

These points all speak to the argument that we should conceptualize transparency in terms of visibility management. If we approach transparency projects as complex communication phenomena we start to acknowledge the practices, dynamics and paradoxes involved. Such an approach theorizes transparency in new, exciting ways and invites us to engage with all the complications involved when states and other societal institutions seek to open up and disclose information.

Governance and Accountability by Transparency

Regulating business is not merely a matter of checking whether individual corporations or entire sectors live up to hard, legal demands or respond consistently to softer pleas for ethics and sustainability. Largely, both harder and softer forms of governance have incorporated transparency as central components. This implies that the equation between more, better information and better conduct has become central to business regulation, and the institutionalization of transparency ideals in governance is well-documented (Braithwaite and Drahos, 2000; Fung et al., 2007). Transparency ideals increasingly underpin most kinds of regulation and governance. Whether you look to the World Bank and its principles for good governance or to emergent trends in global business regulation, transparency is a foundational ideal and aspiration. Such initiatives also take the shape of "regulation by information" (Majone, 1997), "targeted transparency" (Fung et al., 2007), and other efforts to link the disclosure of information to accountability and trust. For instance, a large-scale study of patterns across a wide range of regulatory developments stressed the "triumph of transparency" (Braithwaite and Drahos, 2000) as a primary feature and quality mark of global business regulation. Other principles, such as rule compliance and national sovereignty (Braithwaite and Drahos, 2000), may also be significant, but transparency has gained a strong foothold as the foundation of good and just governance. This makes it all the more important to consider carefully what goes into the production of transparency, and to articulate the complications and limits of transparency as a formula for the betterment of societies. The point is not that we should avoid or limit transparency, but that we need to understand its workings and intricacies if we want to craft better and more feasible kinds of governance and accountability operating in the name of transparency.

One important and increasingly institutionalized shape taken by transparency in the context of governance is the pursuit of accountability. Power's (1997) influential work on the audit society has highlighted how reporting has become a way to position companies as legitimate and responsible. International organizations such as the UN Global Compact contribute to the institutionalization of reporting as a marker of "good" organizations and the development of standardized expectations about the forms and contents of information made available by companies. These formats include reports on corporate social responsibility or sustainability efforts that make it possible to keep track of the performance of individual companies and to compare developments across industries. While regulatory agencies require all kinds of organizations to report on their doings, many reporting initiatives are voluntary and based on corporations' interests in forging and maintaining relations with stakeholders and positioning themselves favorably in the public domain.

In internet companies, reporting mechanisms and activities often take a different and less standardized shape. In a diverse industry marked by large, established tech companies, newer, rapidly growing internet companies and a wealth of very small companies seeking to establish themselves, reporting mechanisms are somewhat patchy and in flux. This implies that what gets reported is decided by the individual company, and that the form in which reporting happens is more or less idiosyncratic. The pressure to disclose information and do reporting often comes with size and market importance, but even some of the biggest internet companies stay clear of standardized reporting schemes developed by others. This allows such companies to decide what to disclose, when to disclose it, and how to make themselves and their practices visible. At the same time, even these self-directed and voluntary kinds of information disclosure take increasingly similar shapes and may lead to the institutionalization of ways of managing visibilities. The focus on controlling information in this industry is highly relevant for the investigation of how the governance of the internet and broader political issues are ordered through the management of visibilities.

TRANSPARENCY REPORTS AND INTERNET POLITICS

In internet companies, reporting takes the shape of transparency reports, a mechanism first developed by Google and more recently adopted by other companies, such as Facebook and Twitter. Such transparency reports aggregate and disclose data about the state of the individual platform. The reports cover issues such as government interferences, including blocking traffic or asking for the removal of content, but also other disruptions of internet services, and security and privacy issues. Transparency reports emerged out of Google's resistance to government interventions in digital spaces. In 2010, the company launched what they called a "government requests tool" intended to make internet users aware of these developments. Drawing on the United Nations' declaration on human rights that "everyone has the right to freedom of opinion and expression" Google presented the tool in the following manner: "we hope this tool will shine some light on the scale and scope of government requests for censorship and data around the globe" (Drummond, 2010). A couple of months later, the company launched the Transparency Reports project, casting it consistently in terms of openness, transparency and the protection of rights to expression. Governments regularly demand certain kinds of information and by unveiling these practices, Google sought to shape discussions of how states control the internet.

These reports are an interesting phenomenon because they do not rely on standardized formats and accountability procedures developed by other companies, organizations or industries. Rather, they set out to provide new approaches to the work of positioning a company vis-à-vis policymakers, regulators and the wider public. They emanate out of a particular conception of what internet companies are and how they relate to states and other actors. Also, they rely on transparency – both as an ideal and a practice of disclosing information – as a way to position these companies as different and particularly committed to securing the benefits of digital transformations for users and societies alike.

Transparency reports deserve attention for other reasons, too. These disclose important information about developments in digital spaces, while also guiding our attention to some issues and not others. Many corporations, Google included, also play a role when it comes to state interventions. For instance, it came as a surprise to many that after the Snowden revelations, Google also disclosed that the company had not been allowed to include information on how it fed the NSA with data on users. These obvious examples of how states seek to control resources and intervene in corporate affairs and private matters were not included in the reports, and this adds to the confusion about what is actually reported in these and similar attempts to account for government surveillance. Google's own account of the limits to what the reports disclosed went like this:

> We want to go even further. We believe it's your right to know what kinds of requests and how many each government is making of us and other companies. However, the U.S. Department of Justice contends that U.S. law does not allow us to share information about some national security requests that we might receive. Specifically, the U.S. government argues that we cannot share information about the requests we receive (if any) under the Foreign Intelligence Surveillance Act. But you deserve to know.
>
> *(Google, 2013: para. 3)*

Like many others, Google found itself entangled in a complex web of decisions about what it could share, what it wanted to share and how to fill the term transparency with meaning.

Transparency reports, like other transparency efforts, are forms of visibility management where decisions about what to highlight and what to downplay are central. These decisions also have more far-reaching consequences, and in the case of transparency reports, they contribute to a very particular configuration of the respective roles and responsibilities of governments and corporations. With the focus on naming and shaming restrictive governments, transparency reports clearly respond to public concerns about government surveillance, such as the NSA surveillance schemes unveiled by Edward Snowden. As Christensen (2018: 165) suggests, such reports cast transparency "as a contestation of state surveillance practices." At the same time, they give companies an opportunity to present themselves as guardians of the internet and a bulwark against states seeking to limit access to information and freedom of expression (Flyverbom, 2016a; Parsons, 2017; Christensen, 2018). Transparency reports set up a particular relationship between public and private forces when it comes to shaping the internet. By focusing on how states limit and interfere in the free flow of information made possible by digital spaces, such reports position internet companies in a very positive light. Internet companies deliver digital promises about open communication and information availability, whereas governments of all sorts come across as the primary forces limiting these possibilities.

At the same time, these reports also serve to make the workings and governance of the internet seeable and knowable. By showing what governments do, these reports offer transparency as a recipe for the world and its betterment, what we may think of as yet another form of transparency evangelism carried out via careful visibility management. But, increasingly, it seems as if the narrative about governments as the main culprits when it comes to limiting free expression and sharing in digital spaces no longer holds up, and internet companies are becoming more aware of their roles as social editors and forces that shape digital spaces (Gillespie, 2014; Helberger, 2016). Recently, YouTube, which is owned by Google, has decided to include information about its own, internal moderation practices in the reports. Such practices, covered in Chapter 4, also shape digital spaces in important ways. However, what we actually get to know through this added material in the reports is hard to decipher. Certainly, social media platforms are sharing more details about how they go about content moderation, but they remain unclear about their responsibilities and willingness to engage with the outside world when it comes to these questions. Along the lines of a focus on managing visibilities, Gillespie (2018a) reminds us, "transparency, even in its candor, is a performance, leaving as much unseen as seen."

Transparency reports forge a strong link between information sharing, accountability and responsibility when it comes to the shaping of regulatory and political concerns in relation to digital spaces. This reconfiguration of public and private responsibilities substantiates the argument that the management of visibilities contributes to forms of social and political ordering in more complex ways than the transparency formula suggests. Questions about the workings of transparency as a source of – and proxy for – accountability point to some of the societal and political implications of the growing importance of visibility management in a digital and datafied age. By disclosing information in strategic ways, companies and other actors not only position themselves in relation to publics and policymakers, but also shape how we understand and act on issues such as the governance of the internet (Flyverbom, 2016a) and the roles and responsibilities when it comes to surveillance and the shape of digital spaces. As the focus on management of visibilities suggests, the consequences of digital transformations extend far beyond surveillance and accountability. As the next section argues, digital spaces also operate as editors of social realities and forces that guide our attention in domains such as culture and politics.

SOCIAL EDITING BY ALGORITHMS AND PLATFORMS

Digital technologies, the internet and social media gained traction with the promise that they would provide more direct access to information, fellow humans, and the world. Possibilities for sharing and interacting would unsettle the hierarchies associated with government-controlled information, elite newspapers and corporate dominance. In contrast to the secret, manipulated and controlled world of the past, the internet and the spread of digital technologies promised to give us access to unfiltered reality, the actual agendas of politicians and peoples' real opinions. While there was a time when these hopes seemed feasible, a lot of what we encounter in digital spaces is of a different nature. Manipulated photos, fake news and staged situations flicker past as we navigate through masses of information, and observed from within digital spaces, the world seems more disparate and divided than ever before. But some digital platforms come across as more pleasant than others. What we often fail to recognize is the kind of work and efforts that underpin and structure these encounters – the management of visibilities at work in social media platforms and the dynamics of attention they produce.

Social media platforms have held onto the argument that they mainly allow us to circulate and give us access to information. For instance, Google insists that it merely organizes the information that is available in digital form, and Facebook tried for long to maintain that it was a technology provider and not a news publisher. For instance, asked whether Facebook had ambitions in the area of news, Mark Zuckerberg (2016) replied "No, we are a tech company, not a media company ... we build the tools, we do not produce any content." But in the eyes of regulators and the public, these arguments do not provide the full story. Social media companies may be technological platforms, but they are also our gateways to information, and what they show us has consequences for what we see, know and are able to control. What we face is the emergence of "privately controlled, public spheres ... [with a] new, data-driven and social form of opinion power" (Helberger, 2016). The fact that social media platforms came to take on such roles as social editors seems as surprising to their founders as the rest of us. For instance, during the US Congress hearings following the Cambridge Analytics scandal, Mark Zuckerberg pointed out that he feels "fundamentally uncomfortable sitting here in California in an office making content policy decisions for people around the world," and that what he "would really like to do is find a way to get our policies set in a way that reflects the values of the community, so I am not the one making those decisions" (Zuckerberg, 2018). The fact that information access and human realities are shaped by the visibility management practices of such companies in largely hidden ways only adds to worries about how to grasp and deal with these developments. Many parts of the automated systems and ways of structuring data at work in digital spaces are hidden and difficult to know about for users (Flyverbom and Murray, 2018). Search results are organized and pushed to users in ways that give them information that they were not even looking for. Try typing in "muslims are," "women are" or "jews are" and Google's autocomplete function will suggest that they are "bad," "evil" and other derogatory adjectives. In reaction to this particular issue, the company states that, "Our search results are a reflection of the content across the web. This means that sometimes unpleasant portrayals of sensitive subject matter online can affect what search results appear for a given query. These results don't reflect Google's own opinions or beliefs – as a company, we strongly value a diversity of perspectives, ideas and cultures" (Cadwalladr, 2016). Google may state that what it suggests are simply the most popular ways to end those sentences, but it is also obvious that search functions are involved in the management of visibilities and part of the ordering of social life. Such forms of curation at play in digital spaces are important to consider because they shape what comes to show up and count as knowledge, and therefore have consequences for the kinds of social ordering that digital, data-driven spaces facilitate.

What is equally problematic is that we have neither the conceptual vocabularies nor the regulatory mechanisms to understand or engage with these developments. As suggested by an emergent stream of critical data studies, datafied, automated systems pave the way for "new knowledge logics" (Crawford, 2016) and forms of governance that deserve scholarly attention (Gillespie, 2017b). We need to consider how algorithms sort data based on what is already popular and visible (Crawford, 2016), and how such decisions come to equate popularity with quality. These operations are difficult to know about, and we cannot see what is chosen and what is left out. But these criteria and decisions are important because they enact choices about appropriate and legitimate knowledge, and "this is the stuff of governance" (Crawford, 2016). It is at the level of such work that the strong link between knowledge and governance is forged through "the ensemble of techniques and procedures put into place to direct the conduct of men and to take account of the probabilities of their action and their relations" (Lazzarato, 2009, quoted in Mansell, 2017). Such questions about knowledge and governance are central in this chapter, because they allow us to articulate the more extensive effects of datafication and managed visibilities. They are also important from a regulatory and political vantage point. When Facebook dodges questions about its role as an editor of social affairs, it is also because regulatory status of a technology platform and a media company are very different (Gillespie, 2017b). These distinctions have extensive regulatory effects, because distributors, such as postal services and internet providers, have no or few responsibilities for content, whereas media companies have extensive responsibilities (Cammaerts, 2016)

The criteria and principles about content policies that internet companies rely on have consequences not only for what is made visible in immediate situations. In a broader perspective, they also shape the ecosystems and formats where we encounter and engage with news and other kinds of content (Flyverbom and Murray, 2018). The organization and editing of content is intimately connected to the way our attention is guided and what we value. If quality is measured by clicks and shares, rather than societal relevance or the nature of contents, it becomes much easier for fake news and sensationalist content to flourish. Shocking or "fun" content will get more attention than other things. You are less likely to click "like" on a post about inequality or the refugee situation, and because the digital platforms are set up to recirculate what is most popular, other types of content are dropped to the bottom. Because algorithmically recognizable (Gillespie, 2017a) information is made visible by digital platforms, we need to understand the logics they are imbued with and the ways they shape culture, politics and society at large. And, as studies of infrastructure have suggested, we need to assess these issues early on, because the infrastructures and approaches we install in digital spaces today are largely invisible and will become even more invisible once they are in place and taken for granted (Bowker and Star, 1999).

ALGORITHMIC TRANSPARENCY AND ITS LIMITS

Digital transformations prompt regulators and citizens to voice their concerns about technical systems, science and related phenomena. Just like genetically modified crops, bioscience and new types of vaccines or treatments have created anxieties and sometimes outcries among the public, and technological developments are subject to public scrutiny and critique. This is most obvious in the area of algorithmic governance and automated forms of decision-making. As we are starting to realize, decisions based on algorithmic operations can be unfair and damaging. For instance, as O'Neill (2016) shows forcefully in her book *Weapons of Math Destruction*, big data and algorithmic approaches to governance and decision-making have wide-reaching consequences and sometimes lead to problematic outcomes. While algorithmic systems may simply be designed to create transparency, they can have unintended consequences. As O'Neill explains, algorithmic decision-making may only intend to measure performance and to ensure quality control. But how performance and quality are measured by such systems may become hard to decipher, and in some cases may mean that the wrong people are identified and punished. Sometimes automated systems make the police pick up the wrong individuals because these decisions are based on data with biases that an algorithm reproduces blindly. And when a Google Photo app automatically tags black people with the label "gorillas," it is because algorithmic decisions are less reliable than they propose to be (Ananny and Crawford, 2016).

How, then, do we initiate conversations about these developments and the possible injustices they lead to? In other areas of science and technology, there is a long tradition for dialogue, multi-stakeholder forums, and other forms of participatory approaches aimed at making developments in science and technology understandable (Singh and Flyverbom, 2016). But when it comes to algorithmic decision-making, the predominant response to the growing concerns about automated approaches to profiling, social sorting and governance has been insistent calls for transparency. Such calls have come from Pasquale (2015) arguing that algorithms are central to the emergence of a "black box society" where decisions about crucial, social issues are made by secretive corporations and opaque technological systems. Increasingly, regulatory, scholarly and public responses to the growing reliance on automation and algorithms have focused on the need for more transparency. How are decisions about money and people made by algorithms? And what kinds of decisions underlie the sorting and editing of digital content we are fed in social media platforms? What are the values and worldviews embedded in technical systems, and how come we cannot simply get access to them – see them, know them and govern them? The transparency formula – that more information will lead to clarity, learning and control – fits well into such ideas: If the public is given ways to scrutinize scientific or technological projects, these systems will be understandable and clear, and the public will be less worried and those involved in the development of science or technology will be held accountable and kept in check. But here, as elsewhere, transparency is not a simple matter, but full of complications and unintended consequences. Also, it may not do much to solve the problem: As Annany and Crawford (2018: 982) put it: "To ask to 'look inside the black box' is perhaps too limited a demand and ultimately an ill-fitting metaphor for the complexities of contemporary algorithmic systems. It sidesteps the material and ideological complexities and effects of seeing and suggests a kind of easy certainty that knowing comes from looking." Also, simply disclosing the specifications of an algorithm does little to our understanding of how outputs are curated. Without the data involved in algorithmic processing, we cannot get an understanding of how algorithms operate. This is why Crawford (2016) suggests that we start from broader and more wide-reaching questions about what kinds of politics algorithms instantiate. As with other phenomena, we need to move beyond focus on algorithms as technical and observable, and also explore the contexts, political spaces and social settings and corporate spaces where they operate.

Questions about transparency enter a wealth of discussions about how to deal with emergent technologies, data and automated decision-making procedures, and the present focus on algorithmic transparency adds another facet to the exploration of how managing visibilities ties in with attempts to govern technological transformations and social affairs.

VISUALIZING REALITY, ANTICIPATING THE FUTURE

As a result of processes of digitalization and datafication, technologies, data and algorithmic operations seep into many parts of social life. The tools and techniques that used to be somewhat contained within social media, search engines or other systems increasingly come to play a role in the governance of social affairs. Citizens can be tracked and rated, as in the Chinese social credit system (Hatton, 2015; see also Hansen and Weiskopf, 2019). Warning systems can monitor and prevent radicalization, terrorism and related security issues (Amoore, 2013). And many other societal attempts to track, document and shape future developments increasingly rely on digital technologies and data-based approaches. These developments raise a number of questions about the potentials, limits and consequences of what we may think of as "algorithmic governance" (Danaher et al., 2017). What counts as knowledge and evidence in such systems, and how are they set up? Who will benefit and who will be impacted negatively, and what happens to principles about justice and ethics? Algorithmic forms of governance rely on automated systems that see the world as data and patterns, and this means that they interpret and treat societal issues and concerns in particular ways. As Morozov (2014) has argued, it makes a huge difference whether we seek to understand and tackle an issue like terrorism through a historical, economic or sociopolitical account of its roots and drivers, or whether we mainly treat it as an information problem. And this is largely what algorithmic governance does: it reduces all kinds of complexities and contextual factors and seeks instead to rely on digital traces as sources of insight. This is one of the promises of data-based approaches to governance: that they will surface social problems and patterns, and offer techniques that make the social world transparent and governable in more effective ways. But we need to consider what happens when governance and politics are treated as data issues, and this is where a focus on dynamics of visibility management has something to offer. Data-driven, algorithmic approaches makes us see, know and govern social affairs in particular ways. To understand these issues, we need to consider both the techniques and logics of knowledge production that algorithmic governance relies on (Hansen and Flyverbom, 2015; Crawford,

2016), and how our attention and governance efforts are guided as a result (Flyverbom, Madsen and Rasche, 2017).

Mappings and data visualizations of various kinds are an important shape taken by contemporary data-driven governance efforts. World maps do not merely show the shapes and sizes of countries and oceans, but also supported the colonization of territories at a distance (Law, 1984). Similarly, scientists seek to map all genes to make human nature legible and to craft possibilities for conquering diseases and otherwise govern health. Cast more directly in terms of transparency, international organizations such as the World Bank and Transparency International spend considerable resources on attempts to develop indexes and mappings of, for example, poverty and corruption. While the drive to make the world transparent may be old, digital technologies allow for new, large-scale attempts to surface, map and govern social affairs. As we are increasingly aware, Google is not only focused on organizing and mapping information in digital spaces, but also the physical world. Google Maps, Google Street View and Google Earth are all involved in ambitious attempts to make continents, cities, streets and houses accessible in high resolution formats. The goals are multiple: people need a good map on their computer or phone, and the more fine-grained and precise, the better. But mappings of where people go and the larger patterns of movement made possible by such services are valuable for anyone seeking to understand human behavior or offer individuals tailor-made services. As a form of transparency project, Google's geolocation services make a direct link between seeing, knowing and governing. If you find out where everyone goes, you also know which routes to suggest, and you may even be able to control where people head next time they need a product or a service. As Zuboff (2019) puts it, mapping and data extraction projects such as Google's are not only about routes, but about routing. Increasingly, your devices will connect what you searched for to mapping services, and tell you where to go next to get what you need. While Google's ambitions in this area are more extensive and wide-reaching than what we see in other mapping efforts, the wish to compile information and govern behavior is central to most projects operating in the name of transparency. The push for transparency is not only about describing and verifying an existing state of affairs, but also about prescribing and performing new realities. These intimate and complex links between seeing, knowing and governing are what the conceptualization of managed visibilities makes central in investigations of transparency projects.

At various times, societies get infatuated with particular ways of accounting for and representing their surroundings. As suggested in Chapter 2, narratives and storytelling have long been forceful ways of making sense of life, past and future. Similarly, numbers and statistics are central to human attempts to describe and understand the world. If we have the numbers and are able to crunch them, phenomena are made legible and knowable. As Knorr-Cetina (1999) has pointed out, an important dimension of knowledge production is the tools and machineries involved, and this also goes for data-driven approaches. Algorithmic governance relies on particular resources and "disclosure devices" that are worth exploring. Data, algorithms and automated sorting procedures have particular characteristics, and are inseparable from the kinds of insights they are used to produce (Hansen and Flyverbom, 2015). The differences between making subjects and objects knowable through narratives or through statistics and big data are immense, and have consequences for what comes to the fore and what is left out of sight. By distinguishing between different disclosure devices (Hansen and Flyverbom, 2015) used to make objects, subjects and processes visible, we get a better grasp of how the production of transparency takes place. It matters to the outcome how visibilities are produced and managed: a number or a statistical representation of an issue such as development or terrorism creates a particular version of what is being observed, and one that is different from a story or a narrative account. This speaks to the issue of managed visibilities: we cannot separate the kinds of visibilities we arrive at from the devices and decisions involved in the making of what comes across as transparency. Transparency is always a matter of making some things visible and concealing others, and this play of shadows is where legibility, knowability and actionability are crafted and complicated. Visibilities are also managed through the institutional classifications and selections at play (Bowker and Star, 1999), and by highlighting the devices, techniques and strategies that go into their production, we realize that they could be different. For example, big data visualizations have emerged as important and popular ways of approaching, capturing and accounting for the world we inhabit. These are often colorful, spectacular, even beautiful, mappings of both extensive and granular data points, such as capturing global cell phone activity, movements in global cities or other large-scale phenomena that produce digital traces and can be sorted and visualized in real time via algorithmic operations (Halpern, 2014; Flyverbom and Madsen, 2015). Increasingly, such mappings and visualizations have become a resource in processes of segmenting, calculating and profiling humans, movements and societal developments. From financial planning and anti-corruption, over policing and intelligence and security efforts, to global development and health initiatives, data visualizations have emerged as an exciting and spectacular new source of seeing, knowing and governing social affairs. The production, circulation and effects of such visualizations is increasingly central to the pursuit of transparency, especially as they promise to do away with well-known temporal problems, such as the time lag between the compilation and publication of data, and ostensibly deliver more accurate, direct and unbiased insights. Such visualizations are part of new modes of managing visibilities via digital technologies and data, and deserve attention because they shape the governance of social and political affairs.

TRANSPARENCY AND SOCIAL PROGRESS

This chapter has highlighted how transparency ideals underpin current attempts to shape political agendas, create new forms of governance and transform politics and societies. We see attempts to advance transparency as a political and societal ideal. Such forms of transparency evangelism play out, for instance, when international organizations seek to advance good governance in the name of transparency, or when internet companies publish transparency reports to show how states limit the free flow of information. Taken together, such approaches work to install transparency as a political and societal norm. Also, transparency takes on a different meaning – as a recipe for the ordering of societies and politics along the lines of information-disclosure, participatory processes and a reliance on technologies that allow for new ways of governing through revelation and visibility. In contrast to the other workings of transparency, these activities involve outward directionalities, where organizational insights, aspirations and orientations are sought transposed to the world outside.

But as argued throughout this book, we cannot separate transparency sharply from other visibility practices and understandings of what visibility implies. Consider, for instance, this variety: At one end of the spectrum, we have Sifry's (2011: 189) diagnosis that more information and the power of the internet is an effective defense against opacity and bad behavior. At the other end, we see widespread fears about surveillance and disciplinary control, such as when Moix (2010) states that "Transparency is a totalitarian obsession. It is the paradise, the horizon of fascist regimes and dictatorships." And then other voices who remind us that the pressure for transparency may lead to very selective types of information to be disclosed, and to increased secrecy and opacity. To make sense of these seemingly conflicting readings of transparency, we need a more encompassing vocabulary that highlights intersections between different ways of governing through visibilities – one that accepts transparency as a fuzzy and malleable ideal. Also, we need to bring out the tensions, paradoxes and entanglements at play in the management of visibilities. As digital technologies and data emerge as infrastructures for a growing number of social domains, processes of disclosing, curating and controlling information become central. Hopes about the transparency formula as a solution to societal and political problems make us ignore this more fundamental development, namely how processes of visibility management seep into the work of running a government, a multilateral organization or political affairs more broadly. Finally, we also need to entertain the idea that transparency is a complicated, possibly dangerous political solution to societal problems: as the focus on managing visibilities suggests, transparency obscures as much as it reveals, and it is rarely possible to actually look into things. As a result, seemingly benign hopes about transparency may end up closing down critique and shifting our attention to masses of information rather than sociopolitical matters and the contexts where they play out.

Transparency is deeply entangled with hopes about societal progress, technological transformations and the institutionalization of novel forms of governance. In such contexts, transparency is translated into recipes for the ordering of societies and politics along the lines of information sharing, participatory processes and a reliance on technologies that allow for new ways of governance through data. By recasting such developments in terms of visibility management, we get a more nuanced understanding of processes of social ordering operating in the name of transparency, as well as the limits and unintended consequences of transparency.

Conclusion: Life in the Digital Prism

This book started from a puzzle. If transparency is not just a simple recipe for the improvement of social life through the sharing of timely and accurate information, then what is it? And how do we make sense of what happens when ideals about transparency, clarity and openness – facilitated by digital transformations – spread through business, politics and societies at large? Our times are marked by a widespread trust in transparency as a panacea and an infatuation with the idea that humans, organizations and societies can be optimized if we can see what they are and how they behave. Through explorations of theories and illustrations, the different chapters have suggested that something more intricate may be at play: that transparency works not like a window being opened on reality, but more like a prism that refracts and produces selective and surprising visibilities. The illustrations also suggests that transparency ideals travel widely, and shape the lives of individuals, organizations and societies in extensive ways. Transparency, as I have put it, is a form of social ordering and a force in the reconfiguration of human realities, organizational processes and politics and society. This implies a view of visibility management as a *fundamental, social phenomenon* shaping life in a digital, datafied world. Also, I have suggested that we can think of visibility management as an *analytical approach* that invites us to conceptualize social processes in new ways. My ambition with this book has been to problematize the direct relationship between digital transformations, more transparency and better governance – what I have termed the *transparency formula*. The shift in analytical vocabulary and approach I have proposed is to make processes of managing visibilities central, and to suggest that a digital and datafied world makes the work of showing, hiding and guiding attention a key concern for individuals, organizations and societies.

So, what happens when hopes about digital-driven transparency trailblazes through the lives of individuals, organizations and societies at large? The responses in this book start from the argument in Chapter 1 that digital technologies and processes of datafication are ubiquitous and infrastructural. This means that we need to understand both how technologies intersect with societal developments, and how societal affairs are handled and recast through technologies, data and automated forms of sorting information and producing knowledge. Social ordering is inseparable from the digital, datafied backbones that make new ways of seeing, knowing and governing possible.

To understand these complications to the simple transparency formula that more information creates more clarity and better conduct, Chapter 2 introduced a conceptual approach that focused on processes of managing visibilities. Rather than providing us with more and better information and leading to more informed decisions, digital transformations create complex and paradoxical situations that require new forms of work, namely visibility management and the guidance of attention. As suggested in Chapter 3, individuals must manage what they show, what they hide and how they are understood, particularly because digital transformations create new opportunities for tracking and profiling that make it difficult to be anonymous and private. In organizational settings, digital transformations and the excitement about transparency lead to new organizational dynamics and new kinds of work that revolve around managing visibilities, and some of these are explored in Chapter 4. Organizations engage in extensive efforts to socialize employees, coordinate activities, document their ways of working and consider how to position themselves. Digital transformations also shape societies and politics, and create a demand for novel forms of visibility management. As Chapter 5 shows, political and societal affairs are recast as data, and the governance of the present and the future becomes largely a matter of managing what is made visible or invisible, or not attended to at all.

Intricate and subtle processes of managing what we can see, know and govern shape the forms of social ordering that play out in the digital prism. As suggested, the dynamics associated with transparency are not so different from other visibility practices. Secrecy also involves intense visibility management and works as a source of social ordering by including some people and things, and excluding others. Staying anonymous, private or opaque in a digital and datafied world is no simple matter, and requires a lot of work to clean up digital traces and manage visibilities. Similarly, surveillance, leaking and other visibility practices all involve extensive work to show, ignore and hide information in strategic ways. Just like purportedly transparent companies also make visitors sign non-disclosure agreements, all sorts of visibility practices seem to entangle with other ones. Also, visibility management serves multiple political ends and a wide range of social functions. Visibility is both an obvious form of recognition and a way to carry out control (Brighenti, 2010; Flyverbom, Christensen and Hansen, 2015). The new visibilities made possible by digital transformations allow for extensive and problematic forms of surveillance, tracking and profiling, but also new forms of resistance and the unveiling of injustices and abuses of power (Thompson, 2005; Lyon, 2015). And sharing lots of information can both be a way to shed light and open up, and a strategy for distraction and "hiding in plain sight" (Stohl, Stohl and Leonardi, 2016). To fully appreciate the significance of visibility management, we need to keep these entanglements in mind. By approaching transparency as a complex and entangled communication phenomenon and a matter of managing visibilities, we are better positioned to engage in discussions about the consequences of digital transformations for people, organizations and societies. These issues are not only theoretical, but also practical and strategic, and certainly political.

STUDYING AND LIVING WITH TRANSPARENCY

The point of this book has not been to suggest that digital transformations are either a liberating force or an oppressive phenomenon.

Digital technologies have become infrastructures for large parts of social life and an increasing number of human activities take a digital form or leave extensive digital traces. We use digital technologies to control global value chains and production processes, to engage in politics and to connect with friends and family. The infrastructures making this possible consist of multiple digital platforms, trackers and other largely invisible ways of sourcing and aggregating data, as well as advanced algorithms and visualization techniques (Alaimo and Kallinikos, 2017; Flyverbom and Murray, 2018). Rather than utopia or dystopia, these developments create new human demands and social forces, and these are particularly about managing visibilities – about what we come to see, know and act on in a datafied world.

Also, we cannot separate digital forms of transparency and other visibilities from questions about what they enable or limit. As Brighenti (2010) has suggested, visibilities are intimately tied to both recognition and control. Being visible means that we are seen and recognized and have a social presence, but also that what we do can be scrutinized and used to shape our conduct. This creates a certain urgency when it comes to curating our traces and managing our presence in digital spaces, because both recognition and control shape what we can do and achieve. Current developments in surveillance, transparency projects, open government and user controls in digital platforms are a useful starting point if we want to understand how digital technologies generate new forms of visibility management. The possible value of using the management of visibilities as an analytical starting point and theoretical framework is the insistence on studying social forces as they intersect with the circulation and curation of information. Questions about visibility management invite us to explore how social life is organized and shaped through attempts to control information and depict a particular state of affairs. In many ways, such work to manage visibilities is at the core of what humans and organizations do. We select very carefully what we share on social media. We invest resources in marketing products and branding organizations. We produce forecasts about future scenarios, craft roadmaps for strategies, and put together sustainability reports and financial accounts (Flyverbom and Reinecke, 2017). All such activities involve extensive forms of visibility management, but are often theorized and studied in other ways. This is partly because theoretical discussions of digital transformations tend to start from elsewhere, such as new technologies on the horizon, the actors and interests at work or the companies and institutions driving these developments (Flyverbom, 2016a).

Many types of studies can be pursued under the heading of visibility management. As I have shown, phenomena such as transparency reports, data doubles and content moderation can be understood in terms of how they involve processes of managing visibilities and guiding attention. But many other phenomena, such as social media, algorithmic governance, digital infrastructures and internet governance, could also be studied fruitfully in terms of how visibilities are managed for purposes of social ordering. Such an approach would bring out novel analytical dimensions and empirical issues that are often overlooked. For instance, how do algorithmic forms of governance cast social phenomena as data points and data visualizations, and what happens to our understanding of sociopolitical contexts and histories as a result? Or how do digital infrastructures spur particular kinds of information flows and priorities that come to shape public opinions? In more concrete terms, doing studies of visibility management may start from broad mappings of visibility practices at work in specific empirical settings; attempts to tease out how seeing, knowing and governing intersect; and reflections on how social ordering plays out as a result. Such studies of the curation of digital traces, the guidance of attention and the governing of social affairs based on digital traces may give us a better understanding of contemporary forms of organization and governance and the way a range of visibility practices – transparency, surveillance, secrecy and leaking – treat social affairs as informational rather than historical or political. In this manner, visibility management may be seen as part of related attempts to grasp bigger questions about the power of digital platforms and the shape of politics and governance in a digital, datafied world.

GOVERNANCE OF AND BY DIGITAL TRACES

Internet companies thrive on our data, engagement and attention, and work hard to keep us active by pushing posts our way, notifying us about "likes" and otherwise reminding us of their presence. Such approaches not only make digital platforms seep into most parts of our lives, but also lead to the production of vast amounts of data about our actions, interests and desires. Increasingly, we are constructed and defined as human subjects by data, and often with particular goals in mind. These may be commercial or political, or about care or control. No matter what, these developments make it necessary for people to manage their digital traces and digital doubles – the digital representations that companies and states rely on when they seek to shape our conduct. Without an awareness of our digital footprints, we may be judged unfairly or miss out on exciting opportunities. Such competencies and literacies are not the first things that come to mind we talk about the need for education and skills development. But without an awareness of visibility management, we are ill-equipped to live in the digital prism.

At the same time, the urgent need to manage visibilities implies an individualization of responsibility. If we are understood, profiled or subjected to control because we fail to manage our visibilities properly, it is largely an individual problem and responsibility. If you apply for a job or a visa, your digital traces will likely be scrutinized. But you are rarely made aware of the negative consequences of not managing your visibilities well enough – in most cases, your visa will simply be refused or the job will be given to someone else with little or no explanation (Hasselbalch and Tranberg, 2016). The curation of digital traces also deserves more attention because they are part of a much larger debate about the structuring of information, the workings of digital spaces and their societal implications (Gillespie, 2017b; Flyverbom and Murray, 2018).

Digital transformations not only set new conditions for the lives of individuals, but also organizations. As social media become important interfaces for communication, digital technologies become backbones in organizational settings and data emerge as increasingly important resources for decision-making. This means that organizations must engage in new kinds of work. On top of dealing with technical issues and skills, organizations have to consider how they depict themselves, and what they do with the possibilities for seeing, knowing and governing that digital transformations afford. Put differently, organizations must manage visibilities carefully when they seek to build a brand, report on their activities, market a product or build relations with customers and stakeholders. The production of representations, spectacles and visibilities is increasingly a core activity in organizational affairs (Flyverbom and Reinecke, 2017).

As a result, key dimensions of what we consider organizations to consist of change shape. Controlling information and organizational processes becomes more demanding, organizational boundaries become porous, and concerns about the inside and outside worlds of organizations move to the fore. Also, visibilities create coordination problems when it comes to communication and socialization. Being observed makes employees act in new ways, and potentially seeing everything makes it necessary for managers to consider what they will do with this information. As in the lives of individuals, managing visibilities becomes an important, but overlooked, part of organizational life and beyond.

Transparency and other visibility practices are also inseparable from bigger questions about politics and societal transformations. This is why we also need to ask ourselves questions, such as "to what ends, exactly, transparency is in service"? (Annany and Crawford, 2018: 985). If the equation between more information and better conduct does not hold up, we need to consider a broader range of outcomes and complications at play when visibility gets connected to political and ideological crusades. Some of these include utopian hopes about technology as a solution and a driver of societal progress (Morozov, 2014), including new possibilities for the shaping of the future through data visualizations. Others involve the dystopian fears that visibility works as a new form of oppression, control and surveillance (Flyverbom, Hansen and Christensen, 2015; Lyon, 2015). To some, visibilities and the corporate access to human lives made possible through data hails a new era of surveillance capitalism and companies that operate in the "reality business" (Zuboff, 2019). Finally, we should not overlook that the push for transparency is both a commercial dream and a state ambition – we can even think of the emergence of a digital-industrial complex (Flyverbom, Deibert and Matten, 2017) seeking to gain perfect information about citizens and customers.

We face a critical junction and "constitutional moment" where largely private actors are installing platforms and infrastructures that disrupt or perform important social functions. As digital technologies become ubiquitous social infrastructures, it makes less sense to think of the internet as a separate domain of society – as a "cyberspace" that is separate, independent, and outside "normal" social life. If more and more parts of social life play out via digital platforms, we need to consider carefully what values and choices they are based on. This is important because with time, they will become so solidified that they disappear from sight. For instance, we have stopped asking questions about the normative underpinnings of the electrical grid or the railway system. Similarly, digital infrastructures will become so natural and taken for granted that exploring how they operate, and questioning what they allow for and suppress will no longer be an obvious option. This is why we need to study and problematize the shapes that digital spaces presently take.

Digitalization and datafication not only give rise to questions about interests and political economy, but also about our conceptions of the phenomenon at the core of present digital transformations, namely data. How do we think about digital data, and what are the implications of different ways of understanding data? While we may agree that data are a potentially valuable resource, it is often unclear how we see and approach this resource. Are digital data raw materials for corporate use? This understanding underpins statements about data as the new oil, and paves the way for commercial uses of data as natural and reasonable. Data can also be understood in terms of private property, and such conceptions are at the heart of data-protection regulation and privacy-focused approaches to data such as those specified in the European Union's General Data Protection Regulation (GDPR). Data can also be seen as a sort of public good. This implies a focus on how societies can nurture and create conditions for the use of this collective resource, such as creating access and the necessary institutional arrangements. How we think about data has consequences for our approaches and responses – in politics, regulation and other contexts. Data, like electricity, will become a central, societal resource. How we get access to and deal with such resources has far-reaching consequences. Just like the decision to rely on coal mines, nuclear plants or sustainable energy sources of electricity has consequences for social life, economies and the environment, so our ways of dealing with data will have far-reaching ramifications for our lives and societies. Life in the digital prism can take different shapes, and we have important choices to make.

By way of conclusion, this chapter has articulated what the conceptualization of transparency as visibility management has to offer – for individuals, for organizations and for society – and for how we think about transparency as a political project, and as a research topic. My hope is that these efforts offer a novel entry point for studies of digital transformations. The significance of digital transformations is not only about the disruption of markets and industries, the size and dominance of internet giants or troubling alliances between corporations and states when it comes to surveillance. Also, while practical and ethical questions about how to handle and use masses of digital data are pressing, they should not be our only concern. As I have suggested throughout this book, to understand the importance of digital transformations, we also need to explore how they influence what we see, know and govern – as individuals, organizations and societies. Digital technologies and data have effects by structuring information, managing visibilities and guiding attention in novel ways. Making sense of these developments remains a conceptual and empirical challenge to be tackled.

Bibliography

Alaimo, C., & Kallinikos, J. (2017). Computing the everyday: Social media as data platforms. *Information Society*, 33(4), 175–191.

Albergotti, R. (2011). Employee lawsuit accuses Google of "spying program." Last accessed September 7, 2018. www.theinformation.com/articles/employee-lawsuit-accuses-google-of-spying-program.

Albu, O., & Flyverbom, M. (2016). Organizational transparency: Conceptualizations, conditions, and consequences. *Business & Society*, 7(3), 43–66. https://doi.org/10.1177/0007650316659851.

Amoore, L. (2013). *The politics of possibility: Risk and security beyond probability*. Durham: Duke University Press.

Amoore, L., & Piotukh, V. (2015). Life beyond big data: Governing with little analytics. *Economy and Society*, 44(3), 341–366.

Anderson, C. (2008). The end of theory: The data deluge makes the scientific method obsolete. *WIRED*. Last accessed September 7, 2018. http://archive.wired.com/science/discoveries/magazine/16-07/pb_theory.

Andrejevic, M. (2013). *Infoglut: How too much information is changing the way we think and know*. London: Routledge.

Andrews, L. (2011). *I know who you are and I saw what you did: Social networks and the death of privacy*. New York: Free Press.

Annany, M., & Crawford, K. (2018). Seeing without knowing: Limitations of the transparency ideal and its application to algorithmic accountability. *New Media & Society*, 20(3), 973–989.

Austin, J. L. (1962). *How to do things with words*. Oxford, UK: Clarendon Press.

Axley, S. (1984). Managerial and organizational communication in terms of conduit metaphor. *Academy of Management Review*, 9(3), 428–437. https://doi.org/10.2307/258283.

Barlow, J. P. (1996). A declaration of the independence of cyberspace. Last accessed September 7, 2018. https://projects.eff.org/barlow/Declaration-Final.html.

Barnett, M., & Duvall, R. (2005). *Power in global governance*. Cambridge: Cambridge University Press.

Bennett, W. L., & Segerberg, A. (2012). The logic of connective action: Digital media and the personalization of contentious politics. *Information, Communication & Society, 15*(5), 739–768.

Berkelaar, B. (2014). Cybervetting, online information, and personnel selection: New transparency expectations and the emergence of a digital social contract. *Management Communication Quarterly, 28*(4), 479–506.

Beyes, T., & Pias, C. (2014). Transparenz und Geheimnis. *Zeitschrift für Kulturwissenschaften, 2*, 111–118.

Birchall, C. (2015). "Data.gov-in-a-box": Delimiting transparency. *European Journal of Social Theory, 18*(2), 185–202.

Birchall, C. (2016). Managing secrecy. *International Journal of Communication, 10*, 152–163.

Boltanski, L., & Chiapello, E. (2005). *The new spirit of capitalism*. London: Verso.

Bostrom, N. (2014). *Superintelligence: Paths, dangers, strategies*. Oxford: Oxford University Press.

Botsman, R. (2017). Big data meets big brother as China moves to rate its citizens. *WIRED*. Last accessed September 28, 2018. www.wired.co.uk/article/chinese-government-social-credit-score-privacy-invasion.

Bowker, G. C., & Star, S. L. (1999). *Sorting things out: Classification and its consequences*. Cambridge, MA: MIT Press.

Boyd, D., & Crawford, K. (2012). Critical questions for big data: Provocations for a cultural, technological, and scholarly phenomenon. *Information, Communication & Society, 15*(5), 662–679.

Brandeis, L. (1913). What publicity can do. *Other People's Money*. Last accessed March 12, 2019. https://archive.org/stream/otherpeoplesmone00bran#page/n5/mode/2up.

Briggs, A., & Burke, P. (2002). *A social history of the media: From Gutenberg to the Internet*. Cambridge: Polity Press.

Brighenti, A. M. (2007). Visibility: A category for the social sciences. *Current Sociology, 55*(3), 323–342.

Brighenti, A. M. (2010). *Visibility in social theory and social research*. London: Palgrave Macmillan.

Brin, D. (1998). *The transparent society: Will technology force us to choose between privacy and freedom?* New York: Basic Books.

Brin, S., & Page, L. (1998). The anatomy of a large-scale hypertextual web search engine. Seventh International World-Wide Web Conference. Brisbane: April 14–18.

Brunsson, N., & Jacobsson, B. (2002). *A world of standards*. Oxford: Oxford University Press.

Brunton, F., & Nissenbaum, H. (2015). *Obfuscation: A user's guide for privacy and protest*. Cambridge, MA: MIT Press.

Cadwalladr, C. (2016). Google, democracy and the truth about internet search. Last accessed October 5, 2018. www.theguardian.com/technology/2016/dec/04/goo gle-democracy-truth-internet-search-facebook.

Callon, M. (1986). Some elements of a sociology of translation: Domestication of the scallops and the fishermen of St. Brieuc Bay. In J. Law (Ed.), *Power, action and belief: A new sociology of knowledge* (pp. 196–233). London: Routledge and Kegan Paul.

Cammaerts, Bart (2016). To avoid mistakes like banning the Napalm girl photo, Facebook needs to start acting like social "media." Last accessed October 5, 2018. www.independent.co.uk/voices/facebook-napalm-girl-vietnam-picture-started-acting-like-media-a7234451.html.

Castells, M. (1996). *The rise of the network society*. Oxford: Blackwell Publishers.

Castells, M. (1997). *The power of identity*. Oxford: Blackwell Publishers.

Castells, M. (1998). *End of millennium*. Oxford: Blackwell Publishers.

Castells, M. (2000). *Network society*. Oxford: Blackwell Publishers.

Cheney-Lippold, J. (2017). *We are data: Algorithms and the making of our digital selves*. New York: New York University Press

Christensen, K. K. (2018). *Corporate zones of cyber security*. Copenhagen: University of Copenhagen, Faculty of Social Sciences.

Christensen, L. T., & Cheney, G. (2015). Peering into transparency: Challenging ideals, proxies, and organizational practices. *Communication Theory, 25*(1), 70–90.

Clegg, S., & Haugaard, M. (2009). *The SAGE handbook of power*. London: Sage.

Clinton, B. (2000). Address by Bill Clinton at Johns Hopkins University, 8 March. Last accessed October 29, 2018. www.techlawjournal.com/cong106/pntr/2000 0308sp.htm.

Cohen, J., & Schmidt, E. (2013). *The new digital age: Transforming nations, businesses, and our lives*. London: John Murray.

Coombs, T. W., & Holladay, S. J. (2013). The pseudo-panopticon: The illusion created by CSR-related transparency and the Internet. *Corporate Communications: An International Journal, 18*(1), 212–227.

Costas, J., & Grey, C. (2014). Bringing secrecy into the open: Towards a theorization of the social processes of organizational secrecy. *Organization Studies, 35*(10), 1423–1447.

Costas, J., & Grey, C. (2016). *Secrecy at work: The hidden architecture of organizations*. Stanford, CA: Stanford University Press.

Crain, M. (2016). The limits of transparency: Data brokers and commodification. *New Media & Society, 20*(1), 88–104.

Crawford, K. (2016). Can an algorithm be agonistic? Ten scenes from life in calculated publics. *Science, Technology & Human Values, 14*(1), 77–92.

Czarniawska, B. (1998). *A narrative approach to organization studies*. Thousand Oaks, CA: Sage.

Czarniawska, B., & Sevón, G. (2005). *Global ideas: How ideas, objects and practices travel in a global economy*. Copenhagen: Copenhagen Business School Press.

Danaher, J., Hogan, M. J., Noone, C., Kennedy, R., Behan, A., Paor, A. De, … Shankar, K. (2017). Algorithmic governance: Developing a research agenda through the power of collective intelligence. *Big Data & Society, 4*(2), 1–21.

De Montjoye, Y. A., Radaelli, L., Singh, V. K., & Pentland, A. (2015). Unique in the shopping mall: On the reidentifiability of credit card metadata. *Science, 347*(6221), 536–539.

Dean, M. (1999). *Governmentality: Power and rule in modern society*. London: Sage.

DeNardis, L., & Musiani, F. (2016). Governance by infrastructure. In F. Musiani, D. L. Cogburn, L. DeNardis, & N. S. Levinson (Eds.), *The turn to infrastructure in internet governance*. New York: Palgrave Macmillan.

Desrosières, A. (1998). *The politics of large numbers: A history of statistical reasoning*. Boston: Harvard University Press

DiMaggio, P. J., & Powell, W. W. (1983). The iron cage revisited: Institutional isomorphism and collective rationality in organizational fields. *American Sociological Review, 48*(2), 147–160.

Drummond, D. (2012). Greater transparency around government. Last accessed September 18, 2018. https://googleblog.blogspot.com/2010/04/greater-transparency-around-government.html.

Easterling, K. (2015). *Extrastatecraft: The power of infrastructure space*. London: Verso.

Economist. (2016). Special report: Companies. Last accessed March 7, 2019. www .economist.com/sites/default/files/20160917_companies.pdf.

Eggers, D. (2014). *The circle*. New York: Alfred A. Knopf.

Eisenberg, E. M. (1984). Ambiguity as strategy in organizational communication. *Communication Monographs, 51*(3), 227–242.

Etzioni, A. (2010). Is transparency the best disinfectant? *Journal of Political Philosophy, 18*, 389–404.

European Commission. (2012). Last accessed March 8, 2019. www.europarl.europa .eu/registre/docs_autres_institutions/commission_europeenne/com/2012/001 1/COM_COM(2012)0011_EN.pdf.

Facebook. (2013). Q2 2013 earnings call. Last accessed March 7, 2019. https://investor.fb.com/financials/?section=quarterlyearnings.

Fenster, M. (2006). The opacity of transparency. *Iowa Law Review, 91*(1), 885–949.

Fenster, M. (2012). The transparency fix: Advocating legal rights and their alternatives in the pursuit of a visible state. *University of Pittsburgh Law Review, 73*(1), 433–503.

Fenster, M. (2015). Transparency in search of a theory. *European Journal of Social Theory, 18*(2), 150–167.

Flyverbom, M. (2011). *The power of networks: Organizing the global politics of the Internet.* Cheltenham: Edward Elgar.

Flyverbom, M. (2015). Sunlight in cyberspace? On transparency as a form of ordering. *European Journal of Social Theory, 18*(2), 168–184.

Flyverbom, M. (2016a). Disclosing and concealing: Internet governance, information control and the management of visibility. *Internet Policy Review: Journal on Internet Regulation, 5*(3). DOI: 10.14763/2016.3.428.

Flyverbom, M. (2016b). Transparency: Mediation and the management of visibilities. *International Journal of Communication, 10*(1), 110–122.

Flyverbom, M. (2017). Datafication, transparency and trust in the digital domain. In *Trust at risk? Foresight on the medium-term implications for European research and innovation policies* (pp. 69–84). Luxembourg: Publications Office of the European Union.

Flyverbom, M., Christensen, L. T., & Hansen, H. K. (2015). The transparency-power nexus: Observational and regularizing control. *Management Communication Quarterly, 29*(3), 385–410.

Flyverbom, M., Leonardi, P., Stohl, M., & Stohl, C. (2016). The management of visibilities in the digital age: Introduction to special section. *International Journal of Communication, 10*(1), 98–106.

Flyverbom, M., & Madsen, A. K. (2016). Sorting data out: Unpacking big data value chains and algorithmic knowledge production. In F. Süssenguth (Ed.), *Die Gesellschaft der Daten: Über die digitale Transformation der sozialen Ordnung* (pp. 123–144). Bielefeld: Transcript Verlag.

Flyverbom, M., Madsen, A. K., & Rasche, A. (2017). Big data as governmentality in international development: Digital traces, algorithms, and altered visibilities. *The Information Society, 33*(1), 35–42.

Flyverbom, M., & Reinecke, J. (2017). The spectacle and organization studies. *Organization Studies, 38*(11), 1625–1643.

Flyverbom, M., & Murray, J. (2018). Datastructuring: Organizing and curating digital traces into action. *Big Data & Society.* https://doi.org/https://doi.org/10.1177/2053951718799114.

Foer, F. (2017). *World without mind: The existential threat of big tech*. London: Penguin Press.

Ford, R. (2003). Against cyberspace. In A. Sarat, L. Douglas & M. M. Umphry (Eds.), *The place of law* (pp. 147–180). Ann Arbor: University of Michigan Press.

Foucault, M. (1969). *The archaeology of knowledge*. London: Routledge.

Foucault, M. (1977). *Discipline and punish: The birth of the prison*. New York: Vintage Books.

Foucault, M. (1979). Governmentality. *Ideology and Consciousness, 6*, 5–21.

Foucault, M. (1988). Technologies of the self. In L. H. Martin, H. Gutman, & P. H. Hutton (Eds.), *Technologies of the self: A seminar with Michel Foucault* (pp. 16–49). London: Tavistock.

Fung, A. G. (2013). Infotopia: Unleashing the democratic power of transparency. *Politics & Society, 41*(2), 183–212.

Fung, A. G., Graham, M., & Weil, D. (2007). *Full disclosure: The perils and promise of transparency*. Cambridge: Cambridge University Press.

Funk, M. (2016a). Should we see everything a cop sees? *New York Times*. Last accessed September 7, 2018. www.nytimes.com/2016/10/23/magazine/police-body-cameras.html.

Funk, M. (2016b, November 20). Cambridge Analytica and the secret agenda of a Facebook quiz. *New York Times Magazine*, p. 5. Last accessed September 7, 2018. www.nytimes.com/2016/11/20/opinion/cambridge-analytica-facebook-quiz.html.

Gabriel, Y. (2015). Glass cages and glass palaces: Images of organization in image-conscious times. *Organization, 12*(1), 9–27.

Galloway, A. R. (2006). *Gaming: Essays on algorithmic culture*. Minneapolis: University of Minnesota Press.

Ganesh, S. (2016). Managing surveillance: Surveillant individualism in an era of relentless visibility. *International Journal of Communication, 10*(1), 164–177.

Garsten, C., & de Montoya, L., eds. (2008). *Transparency in a new global order: Unveiling organizational visions*. Celtenham: Edward Elgar.

Gessler, K. (2017). Facebook's algorithm isn't surfacing one third of our posts and it's getting worse. Last accessed September 7, 2018. https://medium.com/@kurt gessler/facebooks-algorithm-isn-t-surfacing-one-third-of-our-posts-and-it-s-get ting-worse-68e37ee025a3.

Gillespie, T. (2014). The relevance of algorithms. In T. Gillespie, P. Boczkowski, & K. Foot (Eds.), *Media technologies: Essays on communication, materiality, and society* (pp. 167–193). Cambridge, MA: MIT Press.

Gillespie, T. (2016). Algorithms, clickworkers, and the befuddled fury around Facebook trends. Last accessed September 18, 2018. www.niemanlab.org/

2016/05/algorithms-clickworkers-and-the-befuddled-fury-around-facebook-trends/.

Gillespie, T. (2017a). Algorithmically recognizable: Santorum's Google problem, and Google's Santorum problem. *Information, Communication & Society*, 20(1), 63–80.

Gillespie, T. (2017b). Governance of and by platforms. In J. Burgess, T. Poell, & A. Marwick (Eds.), *SAGE handbook of social media* (pp. 254–279). London: Sage.

Gillespie, T. (2018a). Facebook and YouTube just got more transparent. What do we see? Last accessed September 7, 2018. www.niemanlab.org/2018/05/facebook-and-youtube-just-got-more-transparent-what-do-we-see/.

Gillespie, T. (2018b). *Custodians of the Internet: Platforms, content moderation, and the hidden decisions that shape social media*. New Haven: Yale University Press

Gleick, J. (2011). *The Information: A history, a theory, a flood*. New York: Pantheon Books.

Goffman, E. (1959). *The presentation of self in everyday life*. Garden City, NY: Anchor Books.

Goldsmith, A. J. (2010). Policing's new visibility. *British Journal of Criminology*, 50(5), 914–934.

Good, J. (1965). Speculations concerning the first ultraintelligent machine. *Advances in Computers*, 6.

Google. (2011). Passion, not perks. Google newsletter. Last accessed September 2018. www.thinkwithgoogle.com/marketing-resources/passion-not-perks/.

Google. (2013). Government requests for user information double over three years. Last accessed September 28, 2018. https://googleblog.blogspot.com/2013/11/government-requests-for-user.html.

Google. (2017). Google transparency report. Last accessed September 29, 2018. www.google.com/transparencyreport/removals/europeprivacy/?hl=en.

Greenberg, A. (2012). *This machine kills secrets*. New York: Random House.

Hackett, E. J., Amsterdamska, O., Lynch, M., & Wajcman, J. (2008). *The handbook of science and technology studies*. Cambridge, MA: MIT Press.

Hacking, I. (1990). *The taming of chance*. Cambridge: Cambridge University Press

Haden, J. (2013). Inside a completely transparent company. Last accessed September 18, 2018. www.inc.com/jeff-haden/inside-buffer-company-complete-transparency.html.

Halpern, O. (2014). *Beautiful data: A history of vision and reason since 1945*. Cheltenham: Edward Elgar.

Hansen, H. K., Christensen, L. T., & Flyverbom, M. (2015). Introduction to special issue. Logics of transparency in late modernity: Paradoxes, mediation and governance. *European Journal of Social Theory, 18*(2), 117–131.

Hansen, H. K., & Flyverbom, M. (2015). The politics of transparency and the calibration of knowledge. *Organization, 22*(6), 872–889.

Hansen, H. K., & Weiskopf, R. (2019). The interplay of transparency matrices. The example of the Chinese Social Credit System, manuscript presented at EGOS conference, Edinburgh.

Hasselbalch, G., & Tranberg, P. (2016). *Data ethics: The new competitive advantage*. Copenhagen: Publishare.

Hatton, C. (2015). China 'social credit': Beijing sets up huge system. Last accessed October 5, 2018. www.bbc.com/news/world-asia-china-34592186.

Haugaard, M. (2010). Power: A "family resemblance" concept. *European Journal of Cultural Studies, 13*(4), 419–438.

Heald, D. (2006). Varieties of transparency. In Hood & Heald (Eds.), *Transparency: The key to better governance* (pp. 25–46). Oxford: Oxford University Press.

Heemsbergen, L. (2016). From radical transparency to radical discourse: Reconfiguring (in)voluntary transparency through the management of visibilities. *International Journal of Communication, 10*(1), 138–151.

Helberger, N. (2016). Facebook: A new kind of social editor. Last accessed September 18, 2018. http://blogs.lse.ac.uk/mediapolicyproject/2016/09/15/fac ebook-is-a-new-breed-of-editor-a-social-editor/.

Hern, A. (2014). World's most delayed software released after 54 years of development. Last accessed September 18, 2018. www.theguardian.com/technol ogy/2014/jun/06/vapourware-software-54-years-xanadu-ted-nelson-chapman.

Hicken, M. (2013). Data brokers selling lists of rape victims, AIDS patients. Last accessed September 18, 2018. https://money.cnn.com/2013/12/18/pf/data-broker-lists/.

Higgins, V., & Larner, W. (2010). *Calculating the social: Standards and the reconfiguration of governing*. Basingstoke: Palgrave Macmillan.

Hill, K. (2012). Max Schrems: The Austrian thorn in Facebook's side. Last accessed September 7, 2018. www.forbes.com/sites/kashmirhill/2012/02/07/the-austrian-thorn-in-facebooks-side/.

Hilts, A., Parsons, C., & Knockel, J. (2016). Every step you fake: A comparative analysis of fitness tracker privacy and security. Open effect report (2016). Last accessed September 28, 2018. https://openeffect.ca/reports/Every_Step_You_Fake.pdf.

Hofmann, J., Katzenbach, C., & Gollatz, K. (2016). Between coordination and regulation: Finding the governance in Internet governance. *New Media & Society, 9*(19), 1406–1423.

Hong, S., & Allard-Huver, F. (2016). Governing governments: Discursive contestations of governmentality in the transparency dispositive. In P. McIlvenny, J. Zhukova Klausen, & L. B. Lindegaard (Eds.), *Studies of discourse and governmentality. New perspectives and methods* (pp. 149–178). Amsterdam: John Benjamins Publishing Company.

Hood, C. & Heald, D., eds. (2006). *Transparency: The key to better governance?* Oxford: Oxford University Press.

Hosanager, K. (2016). Blame the echo chamber on Facebook. But blame yourself too. *WIRED*. Last accessed September 7, 2018. www.wired.com/2016/11/facebook-echo-chamber/.

Isin, E., & Ruppert, E. (2015). *Being digital citizens*. London: Rowman and Littlefield.

Javis, J. (2009). *What would Google do? Reverse-engineering the fastest growing company in the history of the world*. New York: HarperCollins.

Jeffrey, J. (2008). *Networking futures: The movements against corporate globalization*. Durham: Duke University Press.

Kallinikos, J. (2013). The allure of big data. *Mercury Magazine*, 40–43.

Kirkpatrick, D. (2010). *The Facebook effect: The inside story of the company that is connecting the world*. New York: Simon & Schuster.

Klein, M. (2016). A message from Michael Klein. Last accessed March 12, 2019. https://sunlightfoundation.com/2016/01/04/a-message-from-michael-klein-co-founder-and-chairman-of-the-sunlight-foundation/.

Knorr-Cetina, K. (1999). *Epistemic cultures: How the sciences make knowledge*. Cambridge, MA: Harvard University Press.

Kurzweil, R. (2006). *The singularity is near: When humans transcend biology*. London: Penguin Books.

Lanier, J. (2014). *Who owns the future?* New York: Simon & Schuster.

LaShel, S. (2012). Hate speech in Cyberspace: Bitterness without boundaries. *Notre Dame Journal of Law, Ethics & Public Policy, 25*(1), 279–304.

Latour, B. (1986). The powers of association. In J. Law (Ed.), *Power, action and belief: A new sociology of knowledge* (pp. 264–280). London: Routledge and Kegan Paul.

Latour, B. (1988). *Science in action: How to follow scientists and engineers through society*. Cambridge, MA: Harvard University Press.

Latour, B. (2005). *Reassembling the social: An introduction to actor-network theory*. Oxford: Oxford University Press.

Law, J. (1984). On the methods of long-distance control: Vessels, navigation and the Portuguese route to India. *Sociological Review, 32*(1), 234–263.

Lee, K. (2014). The advantages and workflows of fully transparent emails. Last accessed September 18, 2018. https://open.buffer.com/buffer-transparent-email/.

Leonardi, P. (2011). When flexible routines meet flexible technologies: Affordance, constraint and the imbrication of human and material agencies. *Management Information Systems Quarterly, 35*(1), 147–167.

Levy, S. (2011). *In the plex: How Google thinks, works, and shapes our lives.* New York: Simon & Schuster.

Lippmann, W. (1922). *Public opinion.* New York: Macmillan.

Lister, M. (2018). Facebook ad-targeting options. Last accessed September 13, 2018. www.wordstream.com/blog/ws/2016/06/27/facebook-ad-targeting-options-infographic.

Lyon, D. (2006). *Theorizing surveillance: The panopticon and beyond.* Devon: Willan Publishing.

Lyon, D. (2015). *Surveillance after Snowden.* Cambridge: Polity Press.

Madsen, A. K., Flyverbom, M., Hilbert, M., & Ruppert, E. (2016). Big data: Issues for an international political sociology of data practices. *International Political Sociology, 10,* 275–296.

Majone, G. (1997). The new European agencies: Regulation by information. *European Public Policy, 4*(2), 262–275.

Mann, S., Nolan, J., & Wellman, B. (2003). Sousveillance: Inventing and using wearable computing devices. *Surveillance & Society, 1*(3), 331–355.

Mansell, R. (2017). Our digitally mediated society. In D. Büllesbach, M. Cillero, & L. Stolz (Eds.), *Shifting baselines of Europe: New perspectives beyond neoliberalism and nationalism* (pp. 120–130). Bielefeld: Transcript Verlag.

Marvin, C. (1988). *When old technologies were new: Thinking about electric communication in the late 19th Century.* Oxford: Oxford University Press.

Marwick, A. E., & Boyd, D. (2011). To see and been seen: Celebrity practice on Twitter. *Convergence, 17*(2), 139–158.

Marx, G. (1988). The new surveillance. In *Undercover: Police surveillance in America* (pp. 206–233). Berkeley: University of California Press.

Maurer, B. (2015). How money evolved from shells and coins to apps and bitcoin. Last accessed September 7, 2018. https://aeon.co/essays/how-money-evolved-from-shells-and-coins-to-apps-and-bitcoin.

Mayer-Schönberger, V. (2009). *Delete: The virtue of forgetting in the digital age.* Princeton: Princeton University Press.

Mayer-Schönberger, V., & Cukier, K. (2014). *Big data: A revolution that will transform how we live, work and think.* New York: Eamon Dolan.

McKenna, K. Y. A. (2009). Through the Internet looking glass: Expressing and validating the true self. In A. N. Joinson, K. Y. A. McKenna, T. Postmes, & U.-D. Reips (Eds.), *Oxford handbook of Internet psychology* (pp. 205–222). Oxford: Oxford University Press.

Mehrpouya, A., & Djelic, M.-L. (2014). *Transparency: From enlightenment to Neoliberalism or when a norm of liberation becomes a tool of governing* (No. ACC-2014–1059).

Meikle, G. (2016). *Social Media: Communication, Sharing and Visibility*. London: Routledge.

Moix, Y. (2010). Wikileaks: La transparence est toujours fasciste [Wikileaks: Transparency is always fascist]. Last accessed September 13, 2018. https://laregle dujeu.org/2010/12/10/3872/wikileaks-la-transparence-est-toujours-fasciste/.

Moore, A. (2017). *Intellectual property and information control: Philosophic foundations and contemporary issues*. New York: Taylor & Francis.

Morozov, E. (2014). *To save everything, click here: The folly of technological solutionism*. New York: PublicAffairs.

Mueller, M. (2010). *Networks and states: The global politics of internet governance*. Cambridge, MA: MIT Press.

Mueller, M. L. (2004). *Ruling the root: Internet governance and the taming of cyberspace*. Cambridge, MA: MIT Press.

Mumby, D. K. (2013). *Organizational communication: A critical approach*. Thousand Oaks: Sage.

Neher, W. W. (1997). *Organizational communication: Challenges of change, diversity and continuity*. Boston: Allyn and Bacon.

Newell, B. (2017). Collateral visibility: A socio-legal study of police body camera adoption, privacy, and public disclosure in Washington State. *Indiana Law Journal, 92*(4), 1329–1399.

Neyland, D. (2007). Achieving transparency: The visible, invisible and divisible in academic accountability networks. *Organization, 14*(4), 499–516.

Obama, B. (2009). Open government initiative. Last accessed October 5, 2018. https://obamawhitehouse.archives.gov/open.

O'Neill, O. (2006). Transparency and the ethics of communication. In C. Hood & D. Heald (Eds.), *Transparency: The key to better governance?* (pp. 75–90). Oxford: Oxford University Press.

O'Neil, C. (2016). *Weapons of math destruction: How big data increases inequality and threatens democracy*. New York: Crown Publishing Group.

Open government initiative: Transparency, participation, collaboration. (2013). Last accessed September 13, 2018. https://obamawhitehouse.archives.gov/open.

Orlikowski, W., & Scott, S. V. (2008). Sociomateriality: Challenging the separation of technology, work and organization. *Academy of Management Annals, 2*(1), 433–474.

Otter, C. (2008). *The Victorian eye: A political history of light and vision in Britain, 1800–1910.* Chicago: University of Chicago Press.

Pariser, E. (2011). *The filter bubble: What the Internet is hiding from you.* New York: Penguin Press.

Parsons, C. (2017). The (in)effectiveness of voluntarily produced transparency reports. *Business & Society.* https://doi.org/DOI: 10.1177/0007650317717957.

Pasquale, F. (2015). *The black box society: The secret algorithms that control money and information.* Cambridge, MA: Harvard University Press.

Peters, J. D. (2015). *The marvelous clouds: Toward a philosophy of elemental media.* Chicago: University of Chicago Press.

Power, M. (1997). *The audit society: Rituals of verification.* Oxford: Oxford University Press.

Proposal for a Regulation of the European Parliament and of the Council on the Protection of Individuals with Regard to the Processing of Personal Data and on the Free Movement of Such Data (General Data Protection Regulation). (2012). Last accessed September 7, 2018. https://eur-lex.europa.eu/legal-content/EN/TXT/HTML/?uri=CELEX:52012PC0011&from=EN.

Qualman, E. (2014). *What happens in Vegas, stays on YouTube.* Cambridge, MA: Equalman Studios.

Ravasi, D., & Schultz, M. (2006). Responding to organizational identity threats: Exploring the role of organizational culture. *Academy of Management Journal, 49*(3), 433–458.

Rawlins, B. (2009). Give the emperor a mirror: Toward developing a stakeholder measurement of organizational transparency. *Journal of Public Relations Research, 21,* 71–99.

Ready, J., & Young, J. (2014). Three myths about police body cams. Last accessed September 7, 2018. www.slate.com/articles/technology/future_tense/2014/09/ferguson_body_cams_myths_about_police_body_worn_recorders.html.

Rheingold, H. (1993). *The virtual community: Homesteading on the electronic frontier.* Reading: Addison Wesley.

Ricœur, P. (1990). *Time and narrative.* Chicago, IL: University of Chicago Press

Rindova, V. P., Pollock, T. G., & Hayward, L. A. (2006). Celebrity firms: The social construction of market popularity. *Academy of Management Review, 31*(1), 50–71.

Ringel, L. (2018). Unpacking the transparency-secrecy nexus: Frontstage and backstage behaviour in a political party. *Organization Studies*. https://doi.org /10.1177/0170840618759817.

Roberts, J. (2009). No one is perfect: The limits of transparency and an ethic for "intelligent" accountability. *Accounting, Organizations and Society, 34*(8), 957–970.

Roberts, S. T. (2016). Commercial content moderation: Digital laborers' dirty work. In S. U. Noble & B. M. Tynes (Eds.), *The intersectional Internet: Race, sex, Class and Culture Online* (pp. 147–160). Bern: Peter Lang.

Rogers, E. (1983). *Diffusion of innovation*. New York: Free Press.

Rubio, F. D., & Baert, P., eds. (2012). *The politics of knowledge*. London: Routledge.

Ruppert, E. (2011). Population objects: Interpassive subjects. *Sociology, 45*(2), 218–233.

Russell, S., & Norvig, P. (2010). *Artificial intelligence: A modern approach*. Upper Saddle River, NJ: Pearson Education.

Sahlin-Andersson, K. (1996). Imitating by editing success: The construction of organizational fields. In B. Czarniawska & G. Sevon (Eds.), *Translating organizational change* (pp. 69–92). Berlin: de Gruyter.

Schein, E. (1992). *Organizational culture and leadership: A dynamic view*. San Francisco, CA: Jossey-Bass.

Schnackenberg, A., & Tomlinson, E. (2014). Organizational transparency: A new perspective on managing trust in organization-stakeholder relationships. *Journal of Management, 42*(7), 1784–1810.

Schudson, M. (2015). *The rise of the right to know: Politics and the culture of transparency, 1945–1975*. Cambridge, MA: Harvard University Press.

Scott, C. R. (2013). *Anonymous agencies, backstreet businesses, and covert collectives: Rethinking organizations in the 21st century*. Stanford: Stanford University Press.

Scott, J. C. (1998). *Seeing like a state: How certain schemes to improve the human condition have failed*. New Haven: Yale University Press.

Shapiro, G. (2013). *Archaeologies of vision: Foucault and Nietzsche on seeing and saying*. Chicago: University of Chicago Press.

Seiter, C. (2014). 19 Improvements the buffer team is working on this week. Last accessed September 8, 2017. https://open.buffer.com/buffer-team-improvements/.

Sifry, M. (2011). *WikiLeaks and the age of transparency*. New York: OR Books.

Singh, J. P., & Flyverbom, M. (2016). Representing participation in ICT4D projects. *Telecommunications Policy, 40*(7), 692–703.

Stohl, C., & Stohl, M. (2011). Secret agencies: The communicative constitution of a clandestine organization. *Organization Studies, 32*(9), 1197–1215.

Stohl, C., Stohl, M., & Leonardi, P. (2016). Managing opacity: Information visibility and the paradox of transparency in the digital age. *International Journal of Communication, 10*, 123–137.

Striphas, T. (2015). Algorithmic culture. *European Journal of Cultural Studies, 18*(4–5), 395–412.

Studer, Q. (2009). *Straight a leadership: Alignment, action, accountability*. Gulf Breeze, FL: Fire Starter.

Taplin, J. (2017). *Move fast and break things: How Facebook, Google, and Amazon cornered culture and undermined democracy*. Boston: Little, Brown and Co.

Tapscott, D., & Ticoll, D. (2003). *The naked corporation: How the age of transparency will revolutionize business*. New York: Free Press.

Thiel, P. (2014). Competition is for losers. Last accessed March 7, 2019. www.wsj.com/articles/peter-thiel-competition-is-for-losers-1410535536.

Thompson, J. B. (2005). The new visibility. *Theory, Culture & Society, 22*(6), 31–51.

Thompson, N., & Vogelstein, F. (2018). Inside the two years that shook Facebook – and the world. *WIRED*. Last accessed September 8, 2018. www.wired.com/story/inside-facebook-mark-zuckerberg-2-years-of-hell/.

Thornborrow, T., & Brown, A. (2009). "Being regimented": Aspiration, discipline and identity work in the British parachute regiment. *Organization Studies, 30*(4), 355–376.

Toonders, J. (2014). Data is the new oil of the digital economy. *WIRED*. www.wired.com/insights/2014/07/data-new-oil-digital-economy/.

Tranberg, P., & Hasselbach, G. (2016). *Data Ethics: The New Competitive Advantage*. Copenhagen: PubliShare.

Treem, J. W., & Leonardi, P. M. (2013). Social media use in organizations: Exploring the affordances of visibility, editability, persistence, and association. *Annals of the International Communication Association, 36*(1), 143–189.

Tsoukas, H. (1997). The tyranny of light: The temptations and paradoxes of the information society. *Futures, 29*, 827–843.

Turner, F. (2009). Burning man at Google: A cultural infrastructure for new media production. *New Media & Society, 11*(1–2), 73–94.

Turner, F. (2014). The world outside and the pictures in our networks. In T. Gillespie, P. J. Boczkowski, & K. A. Foot (Eds.), *Media technologies: Essays on communication, materiality, and society* (pp. 251–260). Cambridge, MA: MIT Press.

Vaidhyanathan, S. (2011). *The Googlization of everything: (And why we should worry)*. Berkeley: University of California Press.

van Dijck, J. (2013). "You have one identity": Performing the self on Facebook and LinkedIn. *Media, Culture & Society, 35*(2), 199–215.

Vanian, J. (2016). Why data is the new oil. Last accessed March 7, 2019. http://fort une.com/2016/07/11/data-oil-brainstorm-tech/.

Walters, W. (2012). *Governmentality: Critical encounters*. London: Routledge.

Weick, K. E., & Browning, L. D. (1986). Argument and narration in oranizational communication. *Journal of Management, 12*(2), 243–259.

West, S. M. (2017). Data capitalism: Redefining the logics of surveillance and privacy. *Business & Society*. https://doi.org/10.1177/0007650317718185.

Whitten, A. (2010). *Testimony of Dr. Alma Whitten, privacy engineering lead at Google Inc*. Hearing on consumer online privacy. Last accessed September 28, 2018. https://static.googleusercontent.com/media/www.google.com/da//google blogs/pdfs/google_testimony_alma_whitten.pdf.

Widrich, L. (2017). Introducing the Public Buffer Revenue Dashboard: Our real-time numbers for monthly revenue, paying customers and more. Last accessed October 5, 2018. https://open.buffer.com/buffer-public-revenue-dashboard.

Widrich, L. (2018). Why we have paid, paid vacation and give teammates an extra $1,000 to take time off. Last accessed October 5, 2018. https://open.buffer.com /unlimited-paid-vacation/

Zuboff, S. (1985). Automate/informate: The two faces of intelligent technology. *Organizational Dynamics, 14*(2), 5–18.

Zuboff, S. (1988). *In the age of smart machine: The future of work and power*. Oxford: Heinemann.

Zuboff, S. (2015). Big other: Surveillance capitalism and the prospects of an information civilization. *Journal of Information, 30*, 75–89.

Zuboff, S. (2019). *The age of surveillance capitalism: The fight for the future at the new frontier of power*. London: Profile Books.

Zuckerberg, M. (2016). www.reuters.com/article/us-facebook-zuckerberg-idUSKCN1141WN.

Zuckerberg, M. (2018). Facebook content policy guidelines. Last accessed September 13, 2018. www.recode.net/2018/3/22/17150772/mark-zuckerberg-facebook-content-policy-guidelines-hate-free-speech.

Zyglidopoulos, S., & Fleming, P. (2011). Corporate accountability and the politics of visibility in "late modernity." *Organization, 18*(5), 691–706.

Yegge, S. (2011). Stevey's Google platforms rant. Last accessed October 5, 2018. https://plus.google.com/+RipRowan/posts/eVeouesvaVX).

Index

Printed in the United States
by Baker & Taylor Publisher Services